TWELVE SWEATERS
ONE WAY

Knitting
Saddle Style

✸ To James Murphy, my ninth-grade English teacher in Natick, Massachusetts—wherever you are—for encouraging me to write. You were truly one of the best!

Creative Publishing international

Copyright © 2008
Creative Publishing international
400 First Avenue North, Suite 300
Minneapolis, MN 55401
1-800-328-3895
www.creativepub.com

ISBN-13: 978-1-58923-338-6
ISBN-10: 1-58923-338-7

10 9 8 7 6 5 4 3 2

Library of Congress Cataloging-in-Publication Data
Guagliumi, Susan, 1948-
    Knitting saddle style: a dozen designs for saddle-shoulder garments / Susan Guagliumi.
        p. cm. -- (Twelve sweaters one way)
    ISBN 1-58923-338-7
    1. Knitting--Patterns. 2. Sweaters. I. Title. II. Series.

TT825.G783 2008
746.43'2041--dc22   2007024068
                                                                      CIP

Technical Editor: Judith Durant
Book Design and Layout: Judy Morgan
Cover Design: Creative Publishing international
Illustrations: Heather Brine Lambert
Photographs: Robert Lisak

Models:
Jonathan Bellobuono: page 39
Jessica Benson: pages 33, 71
Amy Cannarella Blanco: page 67
Linda Cannarella: page 45
Laurencia Ciprus: page 55
Adam Clemens: page 79
Olivia Creser: page 63
Tara DellaCamera: pages 75, 79
Travis Flynn: page 29
Ben Guagliumi: page 49
Sydney Marcarelli: page 49
Kristen Senise: page 59
Sofia Senise: page 63

Printed in Singapore

TWELVE SWEATERS
ONE WAY

Knitting
Saddle Style

A DOZEN
DESIGNS FOR
SADDLE-SHOULDER
GARMENTS

Susan Guagliumi

Creative Publishing
international

contents

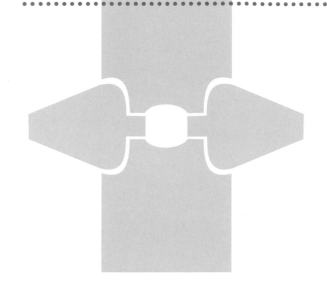

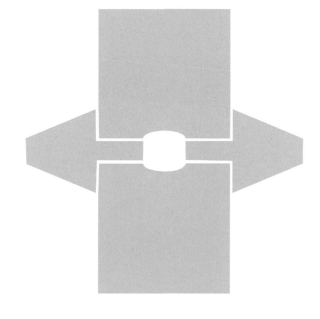

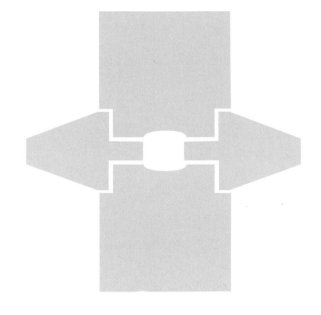

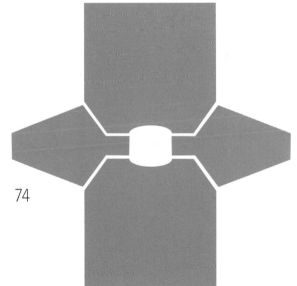

CHAPTER ONE

Knitting Saddle Style

Although the name "saddle style" conjures up images of horses and cowboys and other things Western (and despite the fun I've had naming these sweaters), the term actually refers to a specific way of constructing the shoulders of the sweater.

Basically, in a saddle-style garment, the sleeve cap extends all the way to the neck edge, forming a shoulder "strap." Shoulder straps can vary in width, but they usually average 2" to 4" (5 to 10 cm). The width of the shoulder strap is subtracted from the length of the front and the back pieces of the sweater. The width also contributes to the depth of the neckline.

Traditionally, saddle-style sweaters are based on either a raglan sleeve or a set-in sleeve silhouette. Drop-shoulder, modified drop-shoulder, and sleeveless garments can also be designed with a saddle shoulder. These sweater styles require far less shaping, so the garments are generally a little faster and easier to knit.

Why Knit Saddle Style?

First and foremost, saddle-style sweaters fit beautifully. Even when the garments are oversized, they have a well-engineered fit and look as if they were sculpted to fit the slope and breadth of the shoulders. Because the paired shoulder seams are a couple of inches below the actual shoulder, saddle-style garments contour to the body more easily. The overall effect is smooth and finely fitted.

As an extra bonus, a saddle-style sweater also provides several design opportunities. You can feature special stitches on the strap or carry a textured or patterned effect all the way up to the neckline—as with the cables in Rope Tricks (page 34) and OK Kids (page 48).

Construction and Finishing

Saddle-shouldered garments are usually knitted in four or five pieces (the back, the front or two half-fronts, and the two sleeves). They are worked from bottom to top, although you can also knit the body pieces from side seam to side seam. The stitches run vertically throughout the garment, except at the shoulders, where the saddle-strap stitches are perpendicular to the front and back garment stitches.

The armhole depths of these sweaters are somewhat shorter than you would find in a conventional raglan or set-in sleeve pattern. The reason is that the width of the strap contributes to the length of the sweater body (and the depth of the neckline), and the additional length must be subtracted from the front and back pieces. If the armholes were normal depth, the additional length provided by the shoulder straps would make the armholes far too deep.

Knitting a saddle-shouldered garment is fairly straightforward and not much different than knitting any other sweater that is worked from hem to neck. The way in which saddles really differ from other sweaters is in the finishing.

The main difference in finishing a saddle-shouldered sweater is that, instead of sewing a single shoulder seam, you must join two seams on each shoulder. These two shoulder seams are the most crucial seams in the garment. After you work the shoulder seams, you'll finish seaming the sleeve caps and then join the sleeve and side seams.

The Twelve Variations

This book presents twelve variations on saddler-shoulder sweaters for women, children, and men. Each of the sweater designs is based on a basic silhouette: raglan sleeve, set-in sleeve, drop shoulder, modified drop shoulder, or sleeveless.

The raglan, set-in, and sleeveless styles require the most armhole shaping and tend to have a more definite fit.

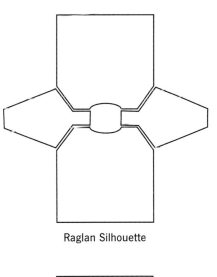

Raglan Silhouette

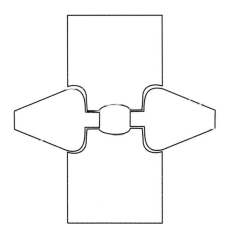

Set-in Sleeve Silhouette

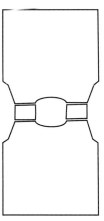

Sleeveless Silhouette

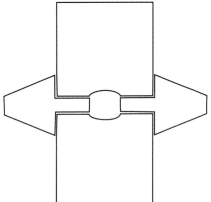

Drop-Shoulder Silhouette

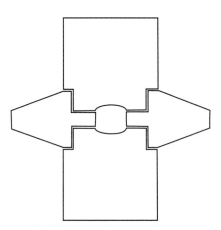

Modified Drop-Shoulder Silhouette

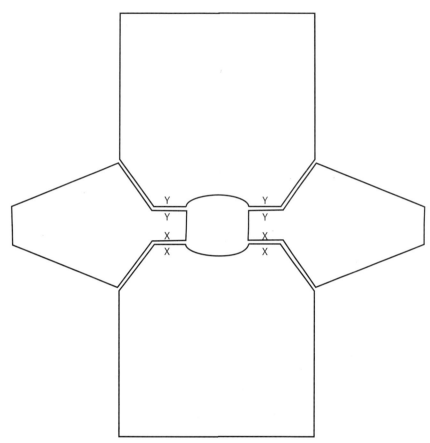

The front and back shoulders of the garment must exactly match the sides of the shoulder straps.

The drop-shoulder and modified drop-shoulder styles require the least shaping and are less fitted styles that lend themselves to oversizing.

For each of the twelve sweater designs, I've provided a materials list, a schematic drawing of the garment's dimensions, a stitch chart for the particular surface texture or fabric patterning, and step-by-step knitting instructions.

Several of the sweaters are sized for both men and women or for both women and children, but even those that are not specifically sized up or down can be altered by shortening or lengthening the sleeves and the body up to the armholes. Begin with the size that has the correct chest measurement to avoid having to refigure the shaping and sizing above the armholes.

In order for the shoulder strap to fit the garment pieces perfectly, all the pieces must be knit to size. The length of the shoulder straps must match the width of the shoulders, as shown in the drawing at left.

The precision of this measurement is key to assembling a perfect saddle shoulder, no matter which of the silhouette variations you choose.

The simplest sweaters are Pinto, the men's crew-neck pullover (page 28), and Prairie, a funnel-neck pullover sized for women and girls (page 62), both knitted in stockinette. The patterns for the rest of the sweaters are easy to follow once you have knitted the first few rows. The stitch work either builds vertically or with a staggered placement. Once you get started, you'll be able to read each row off the one previously knitted, without referring to the stitch chart, so you will be able to work a little faster. The lower border for Rope Tricks (page 32) will require careful attention to the chart, but the patterning on the rest of the body simply repeats vertically.

Although I've suggested adding specific bands, you can substitute different ribs or edgings. Sometimes knitters choose a band based on the look or the way it relates to the stitch work in the body of the garment. Other times, it is a purely structural choice, defining how closely the garment hugs the body.

Some ribs are more elastic than others and will pull the lower edges of the garment in close to the body. K1p1 rib is more elastic than k2p2, which is far more elastic than k6p6. The more stockinette-based stitches there are in a rib (in other words, the more knit stitches that are next to knits or purl stitches next to purls), the less elastic the rib will be. Wide ribs will, however, prevent the lower edges from rolling out or stretching out of shape.

Although it's a matter of personal taste, it wouldn't be a good idea to change the k1p1 rib for Split Rails (page 38) to k2p2, because it wouldn't blend as naturally into the garment as the k1p1 bands that the pattern calls for. On the other hand, if you don't like the twisted stitches in the bands for the Prairie sweaters (page 62), for example, you could substitute wide ribs, garter stitch, lace, or anything else that suits you.

THE TWELVE SWEATER VARIATIONS

Sweater	Style	Silhouette	Gauge sts/rows = 4" (10 cm)	Bands	Stitch work
Pinto	Men's classic pullover	Raglan	20/28	k2p2 rib	Stockinette
Rope Tricks	Women's cabled pullover	Raglan	24/26	None	Cables
Split Rails	Men's V-neck pullover	Raglan	21/43	k1p1 rib	Fisherman's rib
Desert Dreams	Women's cardigan	Raglan	20/26	k1p1 rib	Seeded rib
OK Kids	Children's cabled pullover	Raglan	24/26	k2p2	Cables
Blue Bonnets	Women's pullover	Sleeveless	18/29	k1p1	Twisted and tuck stitches
Rodeo	Women's pullover	Drop shoulder	20/25	Garter stitch	Garter stitch variation
Prairie	Women's/girl's pullover	Set-in sleeve	18/25	k2p2	Stockinette twisted rib
Square Dance	Women's pullover	Drop shoulder	16/22	Garter stitch	Basket weave
Purple Sage	Women's pullover	Modified drop	20/32	None	Garter rib variation
Back in the Saddle	Women's cardigan	Drop shoulder	17/26	k2p2	Seeded rib
Tumbleweeds	Men's/women's vest	Sleeveless	20/24	k2p2	Twisted stitch variation

CHAPTER TWO

Before You Begin

Some processes are essential to all knitting patterns, regardless of the sweater style or the design specifics. You always need to knit a swatch to check your gauge. You also need to be able to follow the pattern directions for shaping, stitch work, and other construction details.

Considering Yarn

Gauge indicates the number of stitches produced with a particular combination of yarn and needle size. Gauge is measured by the number of stitches and rows per inch or per centimeter. Each of the sweater patterns in this book specifies the required gauge and provides information on the yarn used to knit the model garment that is featured in the project photograph.

It is always best to use the yarn that a sweater pattern calls for, but if that yarn is not available, you can probably substitute a yarn that has the same recommended gauge and yardage. This information is usually indicated by the yarn manufacturer as the number of yards/meters per 1.75 ounce (50 gram) ball of yarn and the number of stitches and rows that will knit a 4" (10 cm) swatch. This information provides a good starting point, but by no means does it guarantee that a sub-stitute yarn will work up at the same gauge. Gauge depends on other factors, including how you knit, so be sure to check the gauge of your knitted swatch carefully.

The yarn for the body of the sweater is considered the "main yarn," abbreviated MC (main color). There may also be several contrasting colors in your sweater design. These colored yarns are designated as CC1 (contrast color 1), CC2, and so forth.

Instead of working with a stitch holder, you may prefer to hold stitches with scrap knitting. If you do, choose a yarn that is about the same general thickness as your main yarn, but choose a sharply contrast-ing color so that you will easily be able to see the stitches that you need to pick up. Scrap yarn should always be a smooth cotton or acrylic so it will not leave behind any telltale fuzz when you remove the scrap knitting from the garment stitches.

Check the ball band or skein label for washing directions and always test your swatch for washability. You should also see how the swatch holds up to steaming. Some synthetics should not be steamed at all. If exposed to heat, they are essentially "killed," which means they lose elasticity, causing them to sag and flatten—they can even melt if the heat is just a tad too hot.

The All-Important Swatch

Knitting is based on gauge, which indicates how many stitches and rows form an inch of fabric. The yarn itself is a large factor in determining gauge, but the way a designer uses the yarn and the characteristics of the specific stitch work greatly affect the final gauge.

If you are designing your own knits, there really isn't a wrong gauge. If you like the way the fabric feels, looks, and drapes, the gauge is right. When you are working with another person's designs, however, you have to match the recommended gauge in order for the sweater to knit to size—and to determine the gauge, you have to knit at least one swatch. Think of your swatch as an insurance policy. With just a small investment of time and materials, you are guaranteeing that the sweater fits when all your knitting is done.

Most patterns define their gauge as the number of stitches and rows in a 4" (10 cm) swatch. It's best to cast on as many stitches as the gauge swatch requires and knit the same number of rows—with the hope of knitting a perfect 4" (10 cm) square. Patterns will usually instruct you to knit the swatch in the same stitch you'll use for the sweater.

If the finished swatch does in fact measure 4" (10 cm), you can start knitting. If not, you'll need to switch to a different needle size until it does. If your swatch measures more then 4" (10 cm),

use a smaller needle to get more stitches to the inch or centimeter. If your swatch measures less than 4" (10 cm), work with a larger needle to get fewer stitches to the inch or centimeter.

It is always tempting to stretch the swatch or scrunch it a little so that it measures the required 4" (10 cm), but there really isn't any such thing as "close enough" when it comes to matching gauge. For example, if a 22-stitch swatch is supposed to measure 4" (10 cm) (5.5 stitches per inch [2.5 cm]), then 110 stitches should measure 20" (51 cm). If, however, your swatch doesn't *really* measure 4" (10 cm), look what happens to those 110 stitches:

If your swatch measures	then 110 stitches will measure
4.5" (11.5 cm)	22.5" (57 cm)
4.25" (11 cm)	21.25" (54 cm)
4" (10 cm)	20" (51 cm)
3.75" (9.5 cm)	18.75" (47.5 cm)
3.5" (9 cm)	17.5" (44.5 cm)

If the gauge error is repeated in the front and the back, the body of your sweater could be as much as 5" (12.5 cm) too large or too small and the sleeves will either be overly fitted or sagging. In short, slight discrepancies in gauge can add up to a sweater that just doesn't fit! Stitch gauge not only affects the length of the garment, it also affects the width. So, it's a good idea to recheck your gauge every so often as you knit.

Every knitting pattern suggests needle size for knitting to gauge, but you may actually have to work with a larger or smaller needle to get the stitch and row gauge you need. Everyone's knitting tension is different, and sometimes a person's tension can change from day to day.

Your needles can also affect the knitting tension—both because of the type of material and because needle sizes can differ slightly from one brand to the next.

Circular needles can also produce a different tension than straight needles.

Wood and bamboo needles keep stitches from slipping too easily (a good thing for beginners!) so the knitting gauge tends to be a little tighter with these needles. Plastic, resin, and coated metal needles offer a little more slip. The shiny metal needles often preferred by experienced knitters are slick and fast. Sometimes, you can fine-tune your gauge just by switching from a wooden needle to a metal needle of the same size.

When you have finished knitting your swatch, bind it off. Then, before you measure it for gauge, wash or steam the swatch, just as you would the finished sweater. Always check yarn labels for specific washing instructions, but most wools and blends can be washed or at least steamed by holding the iron a few inches above them.

Many yarns bloom, shrink, or stretch when they are washed. If you do not account for this before you settle on your gauge, you may spend a lot of time knitting a sweater that fits just fine—until the first time it is washed. This step is especially important for cotton yarns. When I work with cotton, I always knit a couple of gauge swatches, including at least one that looks looser than it should. Then I hand-wash and machine-dry the swatches—exactly as I would my cotton sweater—before I measure for gauge. I select the swatch that has the correct gauge *after* it has been washed and dried. If the row gauge before and after is very different, I count rows, rather than measuring, as I work.

Pattern Instructions

Most patterns are written for several sizes. Throughout the instructions, the smallest size is listed first and the increasingly larger sizes follow in parentheses. It's sometimes easy to be confused by all the numbers, so I always make a copy of my pattern, enlarge it, and highlight (with a yellow marker) the numbers or specific instructions that relate to the size I am knitting. For example, when I see instructions to "increase 12 (12, 13, 14, 16, 17) stitches," I highlight only the number that corresponds to the size of my sweater. That way, I know exactly what to do (or how many or how often), without being distracted by numbers that do not apply to me.

The sweater instructions may direct you to do something (for example, increase or decrease) every eighth row a certain number of times, again indicated by a series of numbers. If the directions for your size indicate that you should increase or decrease zero number of times, you can just skip that step in the knitting instructions.

There are several ways to keep track of the specific instructions for your sweater. You may want to make a checklist, keep a numerical tally, or count with a grocery clicker or knitting-row counter. Some patterns indicate how many stitches there should be at the beginning and end of a section of the garment (a sleeve, for example), which makes it easy to double-check that you have made the correct number of increases or decreases.

When knitting a neckline, the directions usually describe the shaping in terms of "every alternate row" or "every other row." As you shape a neckline, you need to knit two rows—one to knit to the shoulder and the other to return to the neck edge. Neckline directions may also read something like "every other row decrease 5 stitches once, 3 stitches twice, then 1 stitch 4 times." You need to knit 2 rows for each decrease or group of decreases—so this shaping will require you to knit a total of 14 rows. The rate of decreasing can vary from size to size, so this is the kind of information you need to highlight for the size you are knitting.

When you need to repeat a set of instructions, the instructions usually begin with an asterisk (★) and are followed by a double asterisk (★★). A series of numbers indicates how often or how many times to repeat the instructions.

Dividing Necklines

When you reach the point where the front of the garment divides so you can knit each side of the neckline, you are just a few rows from finishing the front. Many knitters like to add a second ball of yarn and work both sides of the neckline at the same time, but with so few rows left to knit, I find it is simpler to finish one side first and then knit the other. The V-neck shaping for Split Rails (page 38) is the only exception—because the neckline starts much lower in the front of the garment, I work both sides at once. Although I suggest the following method for working necklines, you can choose whichever method you are comfortable with.

When you reach the point where the work divides, the pattern directions will instruct you to work across a specific number of stitches for the first shoulder or side of the neckline. Then you will bind off the center neck stitches and work to the end of the row. At the end of the next row (and every other row after that), you will be able to bind off stitches at the neck edge.

All of these sweater patterns are charted so that when the neck shaping is done, that side of the neckline is complete. You don't need to do any additional knitting to complete the shoulder, as might be the case with other styles, because the width of the

Decreasing and Increasing

I like to make sure that my increases and decreases are matched so that they slant in opposite directions. To maintain a smooth edge, I always work increases and decreases at least one stitch from the edge of the fabric.

Basic Paired Decreases:

At the beginning of knit rows: Slip 1, SSK (slip, slip, knit). Individually slip 2 stitches from the left needle to the right needle as if to knit them. Then insert the left needle (from left to right) through the fronts of these two slipped stitches and knit them together.

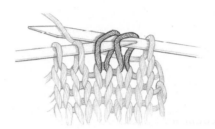

At the end of knit rows: Work up to the last 3 stitches in the row. Knit 2 together, knit 1 (through the back loop).

At the beginning of purl rows: Slip 1, slip 1, purl 1, then pass the second slipped stitch over the purl stitch.

At the end of purl rows: Work up to the last 3 stitches in the row. Slip 2 stitches as if to knit, then return these stitches to the left needle and purl them together through the back loops, knit 1 (through the back loop).

Basic Paired Increases:

At the beginning of knit rows: Slip 1, knit 1. Insert the left needle from front to back under the bar before the next stitch and knit it through the back loop.

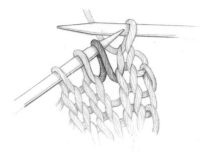

At the end of knit rows: Work up to the last 2 stitches in the row. Insert the left needle into the bar before the next stitch from back to front and then knit it through the front loop. Knit 1 and then knit the last stitch through the back

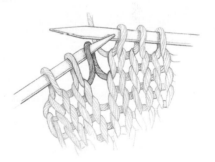

shoulder strap provides the additional neckline depth.

Although you can bind off the shoulder stitches, I prefer "scrapping them off" by knitting several rows of scrap knitting and then binding off the scrap (page 20). You can easily assemble perfect shoulder seams later just by folding back the scrap to work through the live stitches. Also, you don't run the risk that the bind-off will draw in the edge too tightly.

When you have scrapped off (or bound off, if you prefer) the first shoulder stitches, you'll reattach the yarn to complete the second shoulder.

Schematics

Schematics are the road map of a good knitting pattern. These drawings are labeled to indicate how many stitches or inches the various parts of the garment should be. The schematics also provide visual clues as to when and where to increase and decrease.

The schematic is helpful while knitting because it reinforces the written directions. It also supplies the measurements you'll need when blocking the finished garment pieces to size (assuming your gauge was accurate) or when making alterations.

Initially, a schematic can also help you choose which size garment to knit. Pay close attention to the measurements of the garment pieces. Remember that all patterns allow for some ease. The bulkier the yarn, the more ease you need for a comfortable fit. Usually, a pattern assumes 4" to 6" (10 to 15 cm) of ease for most adult garments and 2" to 4" (5 to 10 cm) for children's. If you

are unsure what size to make, measure a sweater that fits well and compare its measurements to those in the schematic.

Each pattern also states the finished width, length, and measurement from center back to sleeve cuff so you can plan ahead for a perfect fit. If you want to change any of the garment's measurements, remember that gauge indicates how many stitches or rows there are in an inch of knitting. You can usually add or subtract garment length (rows) from the body quite easily, but the adjustment will change the number of stitches you need to pick up for cardigan bands and may also affect stitch-patterning repeats. If you add or subtract width (stitches) from a garment piece, you will need to refigure all the garment shaping. So, unless you are comfortable with the math required to rechart your pattern, it is best to start with a size that has the correct chest measurement and limit your modifications to the garment's length.

To adjust sleeve length, you can usually add or subtract an inch or so before the first increase. Anything more drastic than that can be a problem because you will need to redistribute the increases and decreases to retain the shape of the sleeve. Given the choice, it is better to have straight, unshaped areas at the bottom of the sleeves. At the top, they create awkward, square sections that can destroy the shape of the sleeve. (For this same reason, it is always a good idea to check and recheck your gauge throughout the knitting process. Otherwise, you may find that you have made all the necessary increases with many inches still to be knitted.)

Stitch Charts

Unlike row-by-row written instructions, stitch charts give a quick visual impression of the stitches' relationship to each other and the pattern they will form. The charts in this book use standard international knitting symbols and include a text explanation.

Each row of a chart represents one row of fabric (unless otherwise stated), and each square represents one stitch *as seen from the right side of the fabric*. All of the right-side rows are read from right to left. All of the wrong-side rows are read from left to right.

Below is the chart for **stockinette stitch**. The chart indicates that all of the stitches on the right side of the fabric are knit stitches. So, to create this fabric, the stitches in the wrong-side rows must be worked as purl stitches if you are working on straight needles or working back and forth on a circular needle. If you are working in the round, all of the rounds, or rows, would be knitted.

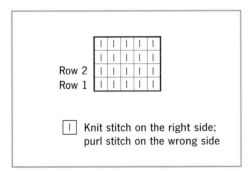

Stockinette stitch

The next stitch chart is for **k1p1 ribbing**. The right-side and wrong-side rows are both worked by knitting one stitch and purling the next, so that purl stitches stack up over purl stitches and knit stitches over knit stitches on each side of the fabric.

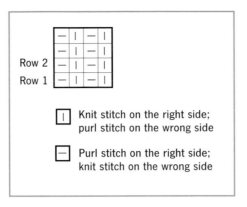

k1p2 ribbing

The third chart is for **garter stitch**. If you are knitting back and forth—on straight or circular needles—garter stitch is worked by knitting every row. As shown in the chart below, the right side of the fabric will have alternating rows of knit and purl. When you work in the round on circular or double-pointed needles, you need to alternate knit rounds with purl to create a garter stitch fabric (circular work is never turned, and knitting every row would produce stockinette stitch).

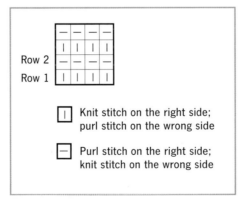

Garter stitch

The diamond and vertical cables in Rope Tricks (page 32) stand out sharply on a background of purl stitches.

Rodeo (page 58) has color changes in the stitch pattern, which are accentuated by rows of garter stitch, forming a smaller pattern of dots.

In Square Dance (page 66), blocks of knit and purl stitches create the illusion of a basket weave.

The stitch chart for each of the fabrics shown at left includes symbols for the unique stitches and techniques used to create that fabric. Don't rely on your memory to keep patterning consistent. It's a good idea to make a copy of the stitch chart for your garment so that you can check off rows as you work and make notes as needed. (You may want to use the original pattern again later for knitting the same garment in another size.)

When increasing for sleeves or for shaping necklines, incorporate new stitches into any stitch patterning as soon as possible, but always maintain one plain edge stitch for seaming (pages 22–23). Also, when dividing the work to knit the front neckline, make a note of the pattern row so that the pattern will match on each side of the neck opening.

For most of the sweaters in this book, you will begin every row by slipping the first stitch as if to purl (that is, with the yarn in front of the needle). You will always knit the last stitch in the row through the back loop, regardless of the stitch pattern. These two edge stitches should never be patterned. Plain edge stitches will help maintain an even, smooth edge that makes perfect seaming so much easier. When you need to handle the edge stitches differently, there will be specific instructions in the pattern notes.

Shaping with Short Rows

The knitting instructions may indicate binding off the center neck stitches to shape the front neckline, but you can also shape the neckline with short rows.

Shaping with short rows preserves the live front stitches, which can be picked up to knit the neckband. This method eliminates the "seam" between the sweater and the band that results when you bind off the front stitches. It also provides a neckline that easily stretches over your head.

This example will help you visualize the short-row process for shaping necklines. Read through it, substituting the numbers for your garment's pattern. Remember, while you are shaping the neckline with short rows or decreases, you may still need decreases at the armhole edges if you are working with a raglan silhouette.

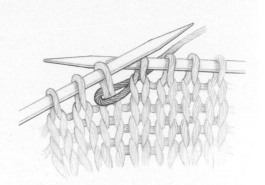

The next stitch on the left needle has been wrapped to prevent a hole when the work is turned mid-row.

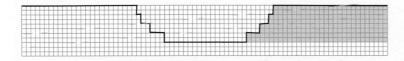

Short-Rowing the Left Shoulder (shaded area)

Row 1: (right-side row) Work across 31 stitches. Wrap the next stitch, as shown in the top drawing at right. (Bring the yarn forward, slip the next stitch from the left needle to the right needle. Return the yarn to the back and return the stitch to the left needle.) Then turn the work over and work back to the beginning of the row.

Row 3: Work across 28 stitches. Wrap, turn, and work back to the beginning of the row.

Row 5: Work across 26 stitches. Wrap, turn, and work back to the beginning of the row.

Row 7: Work across 25 stitches. Wrap, turn, and work back to the beginning of the row.

Scrap off or bind off the 25 left shoulder stitches.

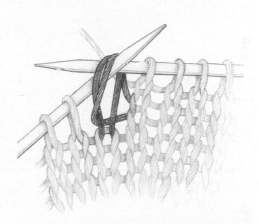

The right needle must be inserted through both the wrap and the stitch it encircles when you knit previously short-rowed stitches in subsequent rows.

Short-Rowing the Right Shoulder (unshaded area)

Work 1 row (right side) across all the stitches on the needle. When you knit the stitches that were short-rowed for the first side, make sure you also knit the wraps together with the stitches they encircle, as shown in the bottom drawing at right.

You will repeat the eight rows you worked for the left shoulder, but the odd-numbered rows are now wrong-side rows. If they are purl rows, move the yarn to the back to wrap and turn.

When the second shoulder is done, work one additional wrong-side row across all the stitches on the needle, remembering to knit the wraps together with the stitches they encircle. Then separately scrap off 30 stitches for the neck and 25 stitches for the second shoulder.

Needles and Notions

You can knit saddle-style sweaters on straight needles or back and forth on circulars. If you choose to use circulars, you'll need 29" (74 cm) for the adult sweaters and 24" (60 cm) for the children's. When you're knitting the sleeves, you'll find that shorter needles are usually more comfortable. Unless otherwise noted, ribs are generally knitted on needles that are two sizes smaller than the main knitting.

Regardless of whether you choose to knit the garment pieces on straight or circular needles, you will still need 16" to 24" (40 cm to 60 cm) circular needles or a set of double-pointed needles. The neckbands for all the pullovers are worked in the round.

Most knitting needle companies also make stitch holders, which come in several sizes and shapes. I have some that look like giant safety pins, without the loop at the end, that stay securely closed. I also like the ones that look like double-pointed needles, with two end caps connected by a spring, because they allow you to remove stitches from either end.

Here are a few notions you might need, too. You won't need all of them for every sweater style, so be sure to check the materials list for each pattern for specific suggestions. Many of these items are things you probably already have in your knitting bag.

- **stitch markers**
- **stitch holders**
- **tape measure**
- **cable needle**
- **crochet hook**
- **Addi Turbo Cro-Needle**
- **tapestry needle**
- **yellow highlighter**

You'll also need some of these supplies when it comes time to block the finished garment:

- **large-head pins**
- **a good steam iron**
- **padded surface that can be pinned into**
- **blocking wires (nice to have, but not necessary)**

CHAPTER THREE

Starting and Finishing

Through my experience as a machine knitter, I have picked up quite a few good tricks for hand knitting. One trick I strongly recommend is using scrap knitting at the beginning and end of the knitting. With scrap knitting, you can retain "live," or open, stitches that you can pick up later for creating bands and edgings.

If you plan from the start, you can also join the live stitches in smooth, bulk-free seams. Live stitches can always be bound off later if you eventually change your mind about the finishing details. I often start with scrap knitting, rather than a provisional cast-on, when I want to work with the beginning edges after I have completed the garment.

I almost always end with two to three rows of scrap knitting because I prefer to join shoulder seams with slip crochet (page 24), a three-needle bind-off (page 91) or, in the case of saddle shoulders, by grafting (page 23). Make sure that the right side of the scrap is on the same side of the knitting as the right side of the main fabric, so the scrap folds back the right way. I always bind off scrap knitting. It may seem like a waste of time to bind off yarn that will ultimately be removed, but the bind-off keeps the stitches snug and secure until

you get back to them—even if the sweater sits in a basket for years waiting to be finished.

Scrap knitting provides an inexpensive, flexible, readily available stitch holder that can accommodate any number of stitches. The scrap knitting is not removed until the garment edge has been seamed, ribbed, crocheted, bound, or otherwise finished and checked. Press the scrap yarn to help it lie flat and then simply fold it back and work through the exposed main stitches. There are many techniques, like grafting invisible seams, that are more easily worked off scrap knitting than directly off the needles.

Always choose a scrap yarn that is close to the same size as your main yarn, contrasts well with it, and won't leave any telltale fuzz when removed. Although I prefer to scrap off my knitting, it's not the only right way to work. If you are more comfortable binding off with the main yarn, by all means, do it that way. Just read through the pattern first to make sure there aren't any finishing details that will require live stitches.

Finishing Considerations

I've always believed that finishing notes should come at the beginning of sweater patterns. The way the sweater is knitted actually determines the ways in which it can be finished. If you choose one knitting method over another, you may find that when it comes time to finish your sweater, you have unintentionally limited your options. So, check all the pattern notes in the instructions for the individual sweaters before you even pick up your needles!

Before you begin finishing and assembling your sweater, secure any yarn tails you will not use for stitching seams. Work the tails back into the knitting, as shown in the drawing below. I usually leave fairly long tails, which can then be used to seam the pieces, thus avoiding the need to start a new yarn just for seaming. To keep these long tails from tangling while I knit, I wind figure eights around my thumb and forefinger and then tie the yarn end around the center of the "eights" to hold the strands together.

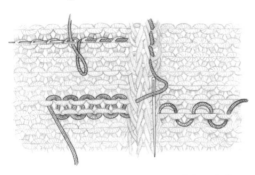

Tails can be worked into the back of the stitches or into the seam allowance.

Blocking

Blocking is an important part of the sweater-making process as it determines the final size and shape of the garment and also enhances the finished look. Although you can sometimes coax the fabric a bit to make up for pieces that are a tad too narrow or wide, don't expect to correct major problems in the knitting by blocking.

Blocking can be as simple a process as covering the sweater pieces with damp towels or holding a steam iron over them and patting them into shape. I block everything I knit to exact size on a large padded surface that has a gridded cover that is marked with 1" (2.5 cm) squares. You can also block knitting on top of an ironing board or several thicknesses of towels or old blankets.

Ideally, you should work on a surface into which you can insert pins. I use pins with large, easy-to-see heads to pin the garment pieces, face down, to the exact measurements shown in the sweater schematic. Then I hold my steam iron about 1" (2.5 cm) above the fabric and saturate the entire piece with steam, without ever resting the iron directly on the knitting. (There are some yarns, however, that specifically require that you "press hard." Scrap knitting also behaves best when pressed flat.)

You'll need a lot of pins when blocking. Space them no more than 1" (2.5 cm) apart all around the piece. You can also work with just a few pins and blocking wires—thin wires that are inserted into the edges of the knitting. Blocking wires make it easier to manipulate large pieces and produce much smoother edges. It takes more time to thread the wires through the edges of the fabric, but the end result is worth it.

When the blocked pieces cool and dry, remove the pins. You'll find that the knitting is much easier to handle. The edges lie flat, the yarn has "bloomed" to fill out the stitches, and the stitches are well aligned. Blocking also guarantees that the sleeve edges or the side edges of both the front and the back are the same length, which is essential when seaming.

About Seams

All garments require some seaming, even if it's only a couple of basic stitches to join selvages, bound-off edges, or open stitches. Always work with a blunt metal or plastic needle to avoid splitting the yarn as you work.

Almost always, I work my increases and decreases at least one stitch from the edge. I never work them as part of any stitch patterning. In this way, I create a consistent seam stitch, which makes it easy and quick to construct perfectly straight seams. If you don't allow for these plain edge stitches, the garment's seams jog in and out every time there is an increase or decrease or a change in stitch patterning. Adding this one trick to your repertoire can make all the difference in how you feel about your finishing!

To **seam selvage edges,** I prefer the invisible seam created by mattress stitch, as shown in the drawings at right. This stitch is always worked on the right side of the garment, regardless of whether the surface of the right side is made up of knit or purl stitches. If you leave a long enough tail when you begin, you can use the tail to sew the seam—which reduces the number of ends you need to hide later. I always work a figure-eight stitch at the base of the seam to align the edges and add enough texture to mimic the cast-on edge. Although a mattress-stitch seam is not the flattest seam there is, it always looks perfect on the outside of the garment.

When seaming knit stitches, pass the needle under two of the horizontal bars between the first and second column of stitches, then exit the fabric. Now pass the needle under two bars on the other

side. Always return the needle to the last place it exited on the opposite side, always one full stitch from the edge (see drawing below). Continue working side to side, loosely seaming about six to eight stitches. Then tug the yarn gently to bring the two edges of the seam together. This technique works better than tightening each stitch as you go—it's easier to see where you have stitched and where you need to stitch next.

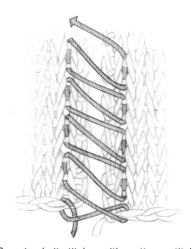

Seaming knit stitches with mattress stitch

When seaming purl stitches, insert the needle into the lower loop of the purl stitch on one side of the seam and into the upper loop of the corresponding stitch on the other side (see drawing below).

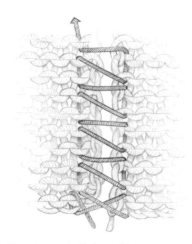

Seaming purl stitches with mattress stitch

Grafting, also called Kitchener stitch, is used to join live stitches in invisible seams. The effect mimics a row of knitting and requires even tension for a perfect finish. You can graft stitches directly from two knitting needles, with the fabric lying flat on a table, but I prefer working from scrap knitting. Press the scrap knitting (not the sweater) and fold it back so that you can see the live stitches. Then thread a needle with a length of the main yarn—at least twice the width of the seam you are grafting—and begin sewing in and out of the stitches as shown in the drawing at right. Each stitch is worked twice because, as you alternate between the two pieces of fabric, the needle always re-enters the last stitch it worked on a side. The shoulder straps for Back in the Saddle Again (page 74) are joined in a nearly invisible grafted seam so that they form a continuous back yoke.

You will need to join the body stitches (whether live on scrap knitting or bound off) to the side (selvage) edges of the shoulder straps. These sets of

Grafting knit stitches

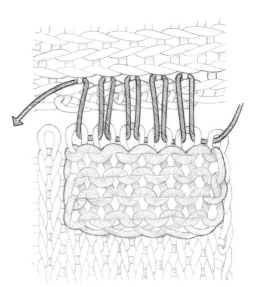

a.

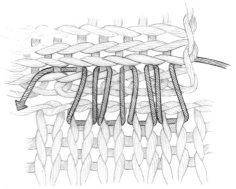

b.

The shoulder stitches are grafted to the side of the shoulder straps, one full stitch from the edge.

(a) If the shoulder stitches were scrapped off, just fold back the scrap to expose the main stitches.
(b) If the shoulder stitches were bound off, work inside the bound-off edge.

stitches are perpendicular to each other and, because the proportion of stitches to rows can be very different, it is important to pin or baste the pieces together before you begin. You may need to stitch more than two bars of the column of stitches along the edge of the strap to balance out each of the garment shoulder stitches. This grafting method does not produce an invisible seam, but it does create a smooth one.

You can also secure bound-off or selvage edges with **backstitching** or **slip crochet**, as shown below.

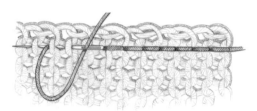

Backstitching a seam

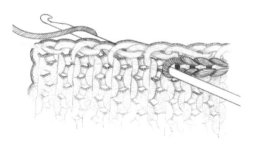

Slip crochet

Picking Up Stitches

Most patterns will tell you *approximately* how many stitches to pick up from selvage edges to create bands. The rule of thumb is to pick up about two-thirds as many stitches as there are rows—although some sources recommend three-fourths as many stitches as rows. Unless you are working a specific pattern stitch or rib, a few stitches more or less won't matter.

The most important things are that the sweater fits over your head and that front bands are not gathered too tightly (because of too few stitches) or flared (because of too many). If you are picking up live stitches from scrap knitting, make sure that you account for every stitch. Be careful not to twist them as you feed them onto the needle. Double-check your work before removing the scrap knitting.

You can pick up stitches either with a knitting needle or a crochet hook. I also have a 32" (82 cm) circular Turbo Cro-Needle (made by Addi), which combines the two (see Sources of Supply, page 93). It has a US 2 (2.75 mm) crochet hook on one end and a US 3 (3.25 mm) knitting needle on the other. You pick up stitches with the hook end and knit them off the other end onto a regular needle.

Afghan hooks, which look like circular knitting needles with crochet hooks (rather than smooth tips) at each end, are useful for picking up a lot of stitches on bulkier fabrics. Knitting the stitches off a hooked end isn't quite as smooth as it is off the knitting needle end of the Cro-Needle, but it works just fine for heavier yarns. When you need to pick up a lot of stitches, these tools simplify and speed up the process.

With the right side facing you, insert the tip of your needle or crochet hook through the edge of the fabric—consistently one full or one-half stitch from the edge—and bring up a loop (see drawing below). Push the loop back on the needle and, working to the left, insert the needle into the next space in the fabric edge. When you have picked up all the stitches, work one plain row and then begin the rib or other band.

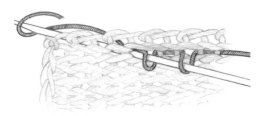

Picking up stitches along selvage edge

Picking up stitches from scrap knitting is easiest if the scrap has been pressed first. The scrap will fold back smoothly, and the first row of live stitches will pop right up. Simply insert the needle through the stitches as shown in the drawing below, so they are not twisted on the needle.

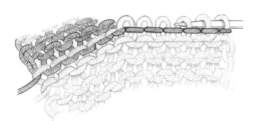

Picking up stitches from scrap knitting

You can knit pockets, flaps, and decorative appliqués directly onto the surface of a garment by picking up stitches across a row or column of stitches, as shown in the drawing below.

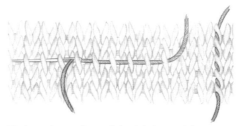

Marking the surface of the fabric to pick up stitches

When you pick up stitches from the neckline of a saddle-style sweater, you will have groups of saddle stitches between the front and back stitches. I usually knit the edge stitch from the saddle together with the edge stitch from the front (for example) to balance out the seam.

You can join seams with slip crochet (page 24), which is worked by pulling up a loop and then drawing it through the loop already on the hook. Make sure that your tension doesn't tighten up the seam and cause it to pull in.

There are lots of ways to approach finishing—and several options for every technique—but with experience, we all find the methods that work best for us. Remember to always practice any new techniques on your gauge swatch before trying them on the sweater itself.

The Twelve Sweaters

pinto

This simple-to-knit stockinette sweater really shows off the characteristic features of saddle shaping. The double neckband is a menswears classic.

Featured Design Variations

- Raglan silhouette
- Doubled neckband

Yarn: Classic Elite "Inca Marl" 100% alpaca with 109 yards (100 meters) per 1.75 ounce (50 gram) skein, 8 (9, 11, 13, 14, 16) skeins of color #1122

Needles: Size US 5 (3.75 mm) and 7 (4.5 mm) straight or 29" (74 cm) needles and Size US 5 (3.75 mm) double-pointed needles or 24" (60 cm) circular OR SIZE TO OBTAIN GAUGE

Notions: tape measure, tapestry needle

Gauge: 20 stitches and 28 rows = 4" (10 cm) in stockinette on larger needle

Sizes: Men's XS (S, M, L, XL, XXL). Model is wearing size L.

Finished Measurements:

Chest measurement: 36 (40, 44, 48, 52, 56)" / 91 (102, 112, 122, 132, 142) cm

Garment length: 22.5 (23, 24.5, 26, 27, 28)" / 57 (58, 62, 66, 69, 71) cm

Center back to cuff: 28.5 (30.5, 32, 34, 36, 37.5)" / 72 (77, 81, 86, 91, 95) cm

Note:
All increases and decreases are worked two stitches from the edge.

Back

With smaller needles, cast on 90 (100, 110, 120, 130, 140) stitches and work 2.5" (6 cm) k2p2 rib. Change to larger needles and work straight in stockinette until piece measures 14 (14, 14.5, 15, 15.5, 16)" / 36 (36, 37, 38, 39, 41) cm from the cast-on edge. Tag the edge stitches to mark the beginning of the armholes.

Decrease 1 stitch at each end of the next and every 4th row 10 (10, 11, 14, 14, 12) times, then every other row 3 (5, 6, 4, 6, 8) times. Tag edge stitches to mark beginning of shoulder slope. Bind off 3 stitches at the beginning of the next 0 (4, 8, 10, 6, 12) rows, then bind off 2 stitches at the beginning of the next 18 (14, 10, 10, 18, 12) rows. Bind off/scrap off the remaining 28 (30, 32, 34, 36, 40) stitches.

Front

Work the front the same as the back until the work measures 5.5 (6, 7, 8, 8.5, 9)" / 14 (15, 18, 20, 22, 23) cm above armhole tags and 72 (78, 82, 92, 98, 102) stitches remain. Continue shaping armholes and *at*

the same time shape the neckline as follows: Knit across 25 (27, 28, 32, 34, 34) stitches, bind off the next 22 (24, 26, 28, 30, 34) stitches and knit to the end of the row. Bind off 1 stitch at the neck edge at the end of the next 3 alternate rows. Bind off or scrap off the remaining 18 (20, 22, 25, 27, 30) front shoulder stitches. Repeat for the left side of the neckline. The neckline can also be shaped with the short-row method described on page 17.

Sleeves

Knit two alike.

With the smaller needles, cast on 46 (50, 52, 56, 56, 56) stitches and work k2p2 rib for 2.5" (6 cm). Change to larger needles and work stockinette until the piece measures 15.5 (16.5, 16.5, 16.5, 17.5, 17.5)" / 40 (41, 41, 41, 45, 45) cm from cast-on edge, *at the same time* increasing 1 stitch at each end of every 8th row 11 (7, 4, 1, 0, 0) times, every 6th row 0 (6, 10, 14, 16, 14) times, and every 4th row 0 (0, 0, 0, 1, 4) times. 68 (76, 80, 86, 90, 92) stitches. Tag edge stitches to mark the beginning of the sleeve cap.

Bind off 1 stitch at each end of every other row 22 (22, 26, 31, 33, 34) times, then every row 2 (6, 4, 2, 2, 2) times. 20 stitches remain for the shoulder strap. Work straight for 3.5 (4, 4.5, 5, 5.5, 6)" / 9 (10, 11, 13, 14, 15) cm. Scrap off/bind off all 20 stitches.

Finishing

Lightly block the garment pieces. Join the front shoulder seams to the front edges of the shoulder straps. Join the back shoulders to the back edges of the shoulder straps. Complete all four raglan seams and the sleeve and side seams. Work in all ends.

With the smaller circular needle and starting at right back shoulder seam, pick up 28 (30, 32, 34, 36, 40) stitches across back neck, 20 stitches from left shoulder strap, 4 stitches along left side of front neckline, 22 (24, 26, 28, 30, 34) across center front neckline, 4 along right side of neckline, and 20 from right shoulder strap. 98 (102, 106, 110, 114, 122) stitches. Work k2p2 rib for 2.5" (6 cm), decreasing 2 stitches in the first round by working 2 stitches together at each back shoulder seam. Bind off loosely using a needle two sizes larger. Fold ribbing in half to the inside and loosely sew in place.

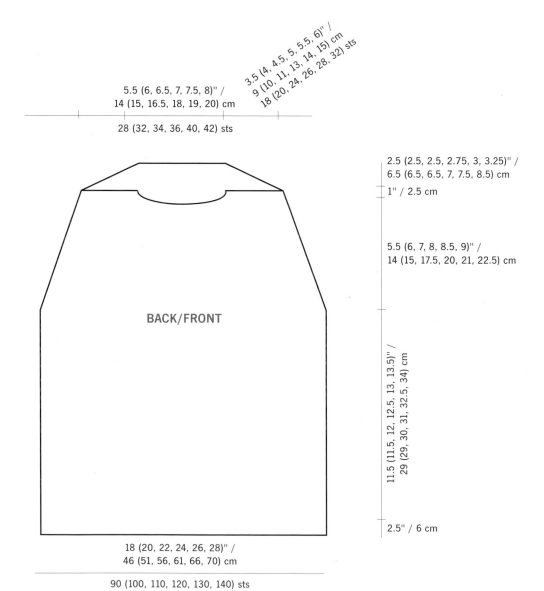

3.5 (4, 4.5, 5, 5.5, 6)" / 9 (10, 11, 13, 14, 15) cm 18 (20, 24, 26, 28, 32) sts

5.5 (6, 6.5, 7, 7.5, 8)" / 14 (15, 16.5, 18, 19, 20) cm

28 (32, 34, 36, 40, 42) sts

2.5 (2.5, 2.5, 2.75, 3, 3.25)" / 6.5 (6.5, 6.5, 7, 7.5, 8.5) cm

1" / 2.5 cm

5.5 (6, 7, 8, 8.5, 9)" / 14 (15, 17.5, 20, 21, 22.5) cm

BACK/FRONT

11.5 (11.5, 12, 12.5, 13, 13.5)" / 29 (29, 30, 31, 32.5, 34) cm

2.5" / 6 cm

18 (20, 22, 24, 26, 28)" / 46 (51, 56, 61, 66, 70) cm

90 (100, 110, 120, 130, 140) sts

Folded Neckbands

Folded neckbands are favored for menswear not only because of how they look but also because they hold their shape much better than plain ribbed bands and are stable enough to support the weight of a man-sized sweater. You can always substitute a folded band for a single band in any pattern.

By the same token, although Pinto has a folded neckband, you can instead knit half as many rows and bind off as usual for a single-thickness band. Alpaca yarn, however, tends to be weightier than wool and somewhat less elastic, so a single band knit with that yarn would have less body than a folded band and may not hold its shape as well.

The directions for Pinto call for loosely binding off the neckband stitches. I find that it is sometimes easier to just scrap off the stitches, fold back the scrap and sew through the live stitches, securing the band to the inside and binding off the stitches all at once.

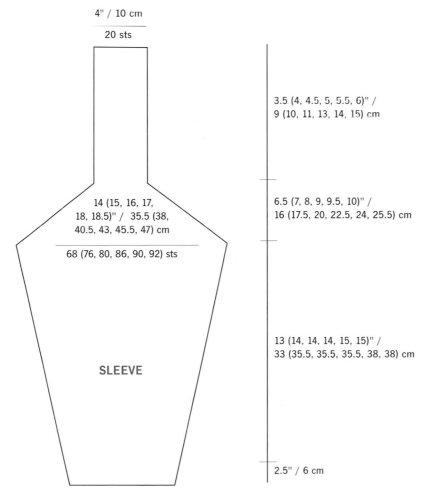

4" / 10 cm

20 sts

3.5 (4, 4.5, 5, 5.5, 6)" /
9 (10, 11, 13, 14, 15) cm

14 (15, 16, 17, 18, 18.5)" / 35.5 (38, 40.5, 43, 45.5, 47) cm

6.5 (7, 8, 9, 9.5, 10)" /
16 (17.5, 20, 22.5, 24, 25.5) cm

68 (76, 80, 86, 90, 92) sts

SLEEVE

13 (14, 14, 14, 15, 15)" /
33 (35.5, 35.5, 35.5, 38, 38) cm

2.5" / 6 cm

9.5 (10, 10.5, 11, 11, 11)" / 24 (25.5, 26.5, 28, 28, 28) cm

46 (50, 52, 56, 56, 56) sts

rope tricks

An elegant diamond arrangement of cables gives way to straightforward, 3×3 cables that cover the body and sleeves of this pullover.

Featured Design Variations

- Raglan silhouette
- Self-finished edges
- Narrow, rolled stockinette neckband

Yarn: Berroco "Ultra Alpaca" 50% alpaca, 50% wool with 215 yards (198 meters) per 3.5 ounce (100 gram) skein, 6 (6, 7, 8, 9, 10) skeins of color #6201

Needles: Size US 7 (4.5 mm) straight or circular needles for the body of garment and 16" (41 cm) circular for neckband OR SIZE TO OBTAIN GAUGE

Notions: tape measure, stitch markers, row counter, tapestry needle

Gauge: 24 stitches and 26 rows = 4" (10 cm) worked over diamond cable pattern

Sizes: Women's XS (S, M, L, XL, XXL). The model is wearing size M.

Finished Measurements

Chest measurement: 36 (40, 44, 48, 52, 56)" / 91 (102, 112, 122, 132, 142) cm

Garment length: 19.5 (20, 21, 22, 22.5, 23)" / 50 (51, 53, 56, 57, 58) cm

Center back to cuff: 28 (30, 32, 34, 36, 37)" / 71 (76, 81, 86, 91, 94) cm

Notes:

(1) Always slip the first stitch in every row and knit the last through the back loop for even selvages. Maintain 1 plain knit stitch at the edges of the sleeve caps and armhole edges and 2 plain knit stitches at each edge of the shoulder straps. Increases and decreases are worked within those edges—never on the edge stitches. (2) You can use a row counter to keep track of the pattern, but I prefer to enlarge a copy of the stitch chart so that I can mark off each row as I knit it. If you draw a line right through each row, it makes it very easy to read the chart for the next row. I usually use a yellow highlighter so that, if necessary, I can still refer back to previous rows.

Back

Cast on 110 (122, 134, 146, 160, 172) stitches and work the diamond cable border, beginning where indicated for each size on the chart on page 34, working the first and last stitches as selvage or edge stitches. When the border is complete, continue working columns of cables until the back measures 11" (28 cm) from the cast-on edge. Tag the edge stitches to mark the beginning of the armholes.

Shape the armholes, maintaining 2 knit stitches at each edge (including the previously slipped first and

The diamond-cable pattern defines the lower edge of the sweater.

Stitch Chart

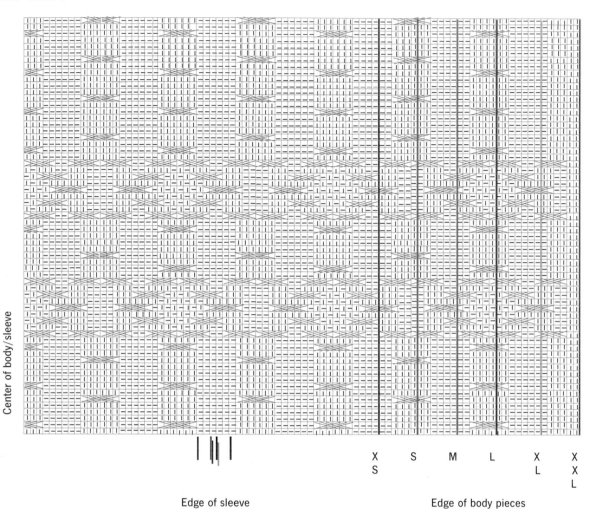

Center of body/sleeve

X   S   M   L   X   X
S   L   X
                              L

Edge of sleeve   Edge of body pieces

*End of diamond border. Repeat pattern as established from this point.

| | Knit stitch on the right side/purl stitch on the wrong side | | Remove 3 stitches on cable needle and hold at back. Knit 3 stitches from left needle, then 3 stitches from cable needle. |

| – | Purl stitch on the right side/knit stitch on the wrong side | | Remove 3 stitches on cable needle and hold at front. Knit 2 stitches from left needle, then 3 stitches from cable needle. |

| | | | Remove 2 stitches on cable needle and hold at back. Knit 3 stitches from left needle, then 2 stitches from cable needle. |

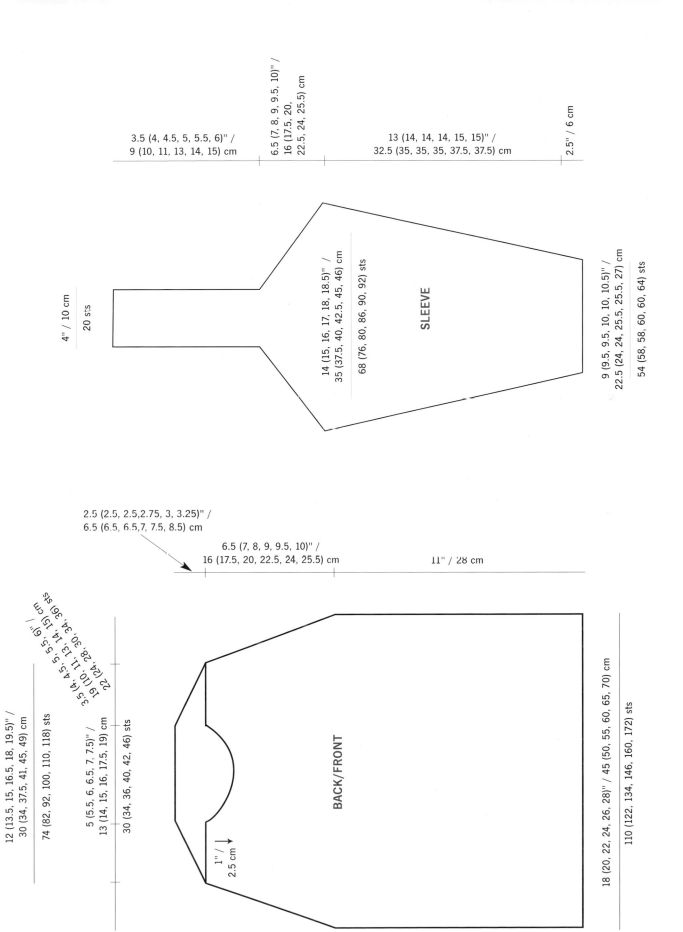

3.5 (4, 4.5, 5, 5.5, 6)" /
9 (10, 11, 13, 14, 15) cm

6.5 (7, 8, 9, 9.5, 10)" /
16 (17.5, 20,
22.5, 24, 25.5) cm

13 (14, 14, 14, 15, 15)" /
32.5 (35, 35, 35, 37.5, 37.5) cm

2.5" / 6 cm

4" / 10 cm
20 sts

SLEEVE

14 (15, 16, 17, 18, 18.5)" /
35 (37.5, 40, 42.5, 45, 46) cm
68 (76, 80, 86, 90, 92) sts

9 (9.5, 9.5, 10, 10, 10.5)" /
22.5 (24, 24, 25.5, 25.5, 27) cm
54 (58, 58, 60, 60, 64) sts

2.5 (2.5, 2.5,2.75, 3, 3.25)" /
6.5 (6.5, 6.5,7, 7.5, 8.5) cm

6.5 (7, 8, 9, 9.5, 10)" /
16 (17.5, 20, 22.5, 24, 25.5) cm

11" / 28 cm

12 (13.5, 15, 16.5, 18, 19.5)" /
30 (34, 37.5, 41, 45, 49) cm
74 (82, 92, 100, 110, 118) sts

3.5 (4, 4.5, 5, 5.5, 6)" /
19 (10, 11, 13, 14, 15) cm
22 (24, 28, 30, 34, 36) sts

5 (5.5, 6, 6.5, 7, 7.5)" /
13 (14, 15, 16, 17.5, 19) cm
30 (34, 36, 40, 42, 46) sts

1" /
2.5 cm

BACK/FRONT

18 (20, 22, 24, 26, 28)" / 45 (50, 55, 60, 65, 70) cm
110 (122, 134, 146, 160, 172) sts

knitted last stitches). Decrease 1 stitch at each edge every 4th row 4 (4, 6, 7, 7, 7) times then every other row 14 (16, 15, 16, 18, 20) times. Tag the edge stitches to mark the beginning of the shoulders.

Bind off 4 stitches at the beginning of the next 0 (2, 8, 10, 8, 12) rows, 3 stitches at the beginning of the next 12 (12, 8, 4, 12, 4) rows, then 2 stitches at the beginning of the next 4 (2, 0, 4, 0, 6) rows. (The shoulders can also be shaped with short rows [page 17], in which case the decreases are accomplished at the *end* of rows.) Bind off the remaining 30 (34, 36, 40, 42, 46) back neck stitches.

Front

Work the front the same as the back, shaping the armholes until 80 (88, 98, 106, 116, 124) stitches remain to begin shaping the front neck. Work across 28 (30, 34, 36, 40, 42) stitches. Join a second ball of yarn, bind off the center 24 (28, 30, 34, 36, 40) stitches, and work across the second side. Working both sides at the same time (or separately if you prefer), bind off 1 stitch at the neck edge every other row. When 22 (24, 28, 30, 34, 36) shoulder stitches remain and the front armholes match the back, bind off or scrap off the shoulder stitches.

Sleeves

Knit 2 sleeves alike. Cast on 54 (58, 58, 60, 60, 64) stitches and work the diamond cable border and then the columns of cables, beginning where indicated for each size on the chart, working the first and last stitches as selvage stitches. *At the same time* increase 1 stitch at each edge every 8th row 2 (0,

0, 0, 0, 0) times, every 6th row 14 (17, 11, 10, 5, 6) times, and every 4th row 0 (0, 9, 12, 20, 19) times. 86 (92, 98, 104, 110, 114) stitches. Work until the sleeve measures 15.5 (16.5, 16.5, 16.5, 17.5, 17.5)" / 39 (42, 42, 42, 44, 44) cm from the cast-on edge. Tag the edge stitches to mark the beginning of the sleeve cap.

Maintaining 2 knit stitches at each edge, shape the sleeve cap by decreasing 1 stitch at each edge every other row 11 (14, 17, 18, 19, 21) times, then every row 20 (20, 20, 22, 24, 24) times. 24 stitches remain. Tag the edge stitches to mark the beginning of the shoulder strap.

Maintaining 3 knit stitches at each edge (2 knit stitches in addition to the slipped first or knitted last stitches), continue the cable pattern until the strap measures 3.5 (4, 4.5, 5, 5.5, 6)" / 9 (10, 11, 13, 14, 15) cm from the top of the sleeve cap. Bind off all 24 stitches.

Finishing

With the neck edges even and working 1 stitch from the edge of the straps, join the front shoulders to one side edge of each shoulder strap. Use the edge tags to help position the pieces exactly. Join the back shoulders to the remaining strap edges. Working 1 stitch from the edge, sew all four armhole/sleeve cap seams. Sew sleeve and side seams. Work in all tails.

With a 16" (41 cm) circular needle (or with double-pointed needles) and the right side of the garment facing you, pick up approximately 80 (80, 80, 86, 86, 86) stitches. Purl 2 rows and then bind off loosely.

Wash the finished garment and lay flat to dry. This step will help set the stitches and add depth to the cables.

I-Cord Edging

You can finish the neck of Rope Tricks with an I-cord edging. This is a handy finish to know whenever you want an alternative to rib.

Plain I-cord is knitted on two short double-pointed needles over 3 or 4 stitches. At the end of each row, instead of turning the work over, the stitches are slid back to the end of the needle and the yarn loops across the back of them. As the piece lengthens, the loops are absorbed into the stitches and a perfectly round cord emerges. When worked on more than 4 stitches, the loops don't completely disappear and the cord flattens somewhat, but it still produces a nice smooth cord.

Taking it one step further, you can pick up the edge of a garment (live or bound off) and attach the I-cord as you knit it. First, with a pair of double-pointed needles, cast on 3 stitches for the cord. Then, with the right side of the garment facing you, pick up the edge on a circular needle, usually beginning at a seam. Hold the double-pointed needle next to the circular needle as you work. *Knit 2, slip 1 (on the double-pointed needles) then knit 1 stitch from the circular needle. Pass the slipped stitch over the last knit stitch and, with the yarn in back, slide all 3 stitches to the right end of the double-pointed needle.** Repeat * to **.

As you work, the yarn always slips behind the 3 stitches on the double-pointed needle, forming the I-cord as the live stitches on the circular needle are bound off, one by one. Hold the work on your lap so that the weight of the sweater is supported. You will hold the double-pointed needles while you work the I-cord and only intermittently hold the circular needle when you knit the 1 stitch and pass the slipped stitch over it. Working with three needles (the circular needle and a pair of double-points) may seem awkward at first, but you will develop a rhythm as the work progresses. When you reach the end of the stitches on the circular needle, you can bind off the end of the I-cord or graft the stitches to the beginning of the cord for a nearly seamless finish

The same method works for attaching narrow bands of garter stitch, bias, or lace. As long as you can hold the working needles alongside the needle that is holding the garment stitches, you can always combine the two sets of stitches. If the garment stitches are live, rather than a picked-up edge, they are also bound off in the process.

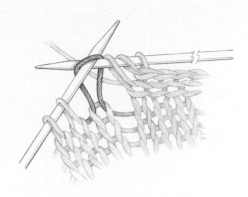

Knit 2 stitches of the I-cord (on double-pointed needles), slip the 3rd stitch and then knit 1 stitch from the garment edge.

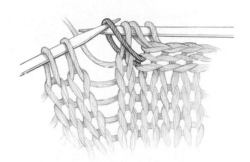

There are now 4 stitches on the double-pointed needle. Pass the 3rd stitch over the 4th stitch (the one knitted from the garment edge).

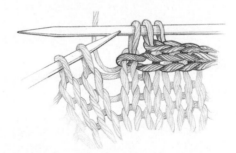

The I-cord has been attached to the edge of the garment. Knit 1 or 2 more "rows" on the I-cord and then repeat the first two steps. The edge may not need to be worked with every row of the I-cord.

split rails

The Fisherman Rib pattern, sometimes called English Rib, is a tuck-stitch variation of k1p1 rib. It creates a lofty, textured fabric. Although the tucks are executed on the wrong side of the fabric, the full effect is visible on the reverse side, which is the right side.

Featured Design Variations

- Raglan silhouette
- k1p1 rib bands blend seamlessly into Fisherman Rib pattern
- Mitered V-neckband

Yarn: Rowan "Felted Tweed" 50% merino wool, 25% alpaca, and 25% viscose with 191 yards (175 meters) per 1.75 ounce (50 gram) ball, color #141 (Whisper) 8 (9, 10, 12, 14, 16) balls

Needles: Size US 2 (2.75 mm) 24" (60 cm) and 29" (74 cm) and Size US 4 (3.5 mm) straight or circular needles OR SIZE TO OBTAIN GAUGE

Notions: tapestry needle, tape measure, stitch markers

Gauge: 21 stitches and 43 rows = 4" (10 cm) in Fisherman Rib pattern on larger needles

Sizes: Men's XS (S, M, L, XL, XXL). Model is wearing size M.

Finished Measurements

Chest measurement: 36 (40, 44, 48, 52, 56)" / 91 (102, 112, 122, 132, 142) cm

Garment length: 24 (24.5, 26, 27.5, 29, 30)" / 61 (62, 66, 70, 74, 76) cm

Center back to cuff: 28.5 (30.5, 32, 34, 36, 37.5)" / 72 (77, 81, 86, 91, 95) cm

Notes: (1) Work all increases and decreases 2 (knit) stitches from the edge and maintain 2 plain edge stitches on shoulder straps. These 2 stitches include the slipped first stitch and knitted last stitch of every row. (2) Make a checklist to keep track of the armhole and neckline decreases for the front.

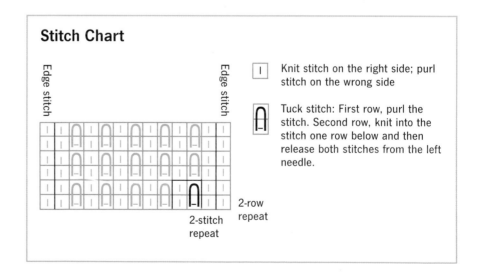

Stitch Chart

Edge stitch

Edge stitch

2-stitch repeat

2-row repeat

| | Knit stitch on the right side; purl stitch on the wrong side |

Tuck stitch: First row, purl the stitch. Second row, knit into the stitch one row below and then release both stitches from the left needle.

Working decreases two stitches from the edge forms a decorative seam line.

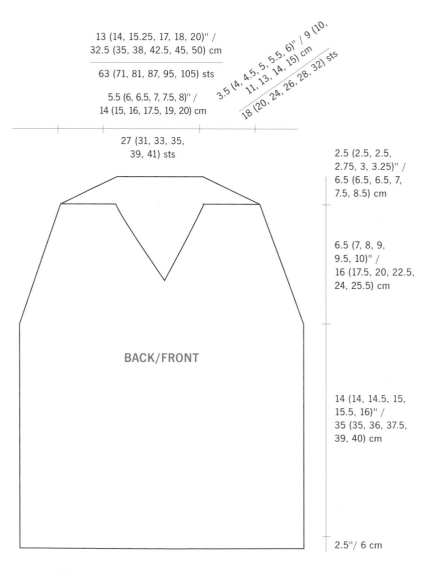

13 (14, 15.25, 17, 18, 20)" /
32.5 (35, 38, 42.5, 45, 50) cm

63 (71, 81, 87, 95, 105) sts

5.5 (6, 6.5, 7, 7.5, 8)" /
14 (15, 16, 17.5, 19, 20) cm

3.5 (4, 4.5, 5, 5.5, 6)" / 9 (10,
11, 13, 14, 15) cm

18 (20, 24, 26, 28, 32) sts

27 (31, 33, 35,
39, 41) sts

2.5 (2.5, 2.5,
2.75, 3, 3.25)" /
6.5 (6.5, 6.5, 7,
7.5, 8.5) cm

6.5 (7, 8, 9,
9.5, 10)" /
16 (17.5, 20, 22.5,
24, 25.5) cm

BACK/FRONT

14 (14, 14.5, 15,
15.5, 16)" /
35 (35, 36, 37.5,
39, 40) cm

2.5"/ 6 cm

18 (20, 22, 24, 26, 28)" / 45 (50, 55, 60, 65, 70) cm

95 (105, 115, 127, 137, 149) sts

Back

With smaller needles, cast on 95 (105, 115, 127, 137, 149) stitches and work k1p1 rib for 2.5" (6 cm). Change to larger needle and work Fisherman Rib pattern until piece measures 16.5 (16.5, 17, 17.5, 18, 18.5)" / 42 (42, 43, 44, 46, 47) cm from cast-on edge. Tag edge stitches to mark beginning of armhole.

Working 2 stitches from the edge of the fabric, decrease 1 stitch at each end of the next and every 6th right side row 1 (2, 7, 6, 7, 7) times, then every 4th row 14 (14, 9, 13, 13, 14) times. 63 (71, 81, 87, 95, 105) stitches. Work 1 wrong side row and then tag the edge stitches to mark the beginning of the shoulder. Bind off 4 stitches at the beginning of the next 0 (4, 12, 10, 14, 16) rows, then bind off 3 stitches at the beginning of the next 12 (8, 0, 4, 0, 0) rows. End with a right-side row. Scrap off, bind off, or place on a holder the remaining 27 (31, 33, 35, 39, 41) center back neck stitches.

Front

Work same as back to beginning of armholes. Work armholes as for back *at the same time*. When work measures 2" (5 cm) above beginning of armholes, begin working both sides of the front neckline as follows. Work across 47 (52, 57, 63, 68, 74) stitches, knit 2 stitches together, and work to the end of the row. Next row, work to the center and attach a second ball of yarn to work both sides of the neckline at the same time. Maintaining 2 knit stitches at each neckline edge, decrease 1 stitch at the neckline every 6th row 0 (0, 0, 2, 1, 1) times, every 4th row 10 (11, 15, 15, 18, 19) times, and every alternate row 3 (4, 1, 0, 0, 0). End with a right-side row. When the piece measures 6.5 (7, 8, 9, 9.5, 10)" / 17 (18, 20, 23, 24, 25) cm above armhole tag, scrap off or bind off the remaining 18 (20, 24, 26, 28, 32) shoulder stitches. (Note that the decreases on left side of the neckline will be made at the end of right-side rows and those on the right side of the neckline at the beginning of right-side rows.)

Sleeves

Knit two alike. With smaller needles, cast on 47 (49, 49, 51, 51, 53) stitches and work k1p1 rib for 2.5" (6 cm). Change to larger needles and work sleeve in pattern for 13 (14, 14, 14, 15, 15)" / 33 (36, 36, 36, 38, 38) cm above ribbing, *at the same time* increasing 1 stitch each end of every 10th row 10 (7, 5, 0, 0, 0) times, every 8th row 3 (8, 17, 11, 7, 7) times, then every 6th row 0 (0, 0, 8, 15, 15) times. 73 (79, 83, 89, 95,

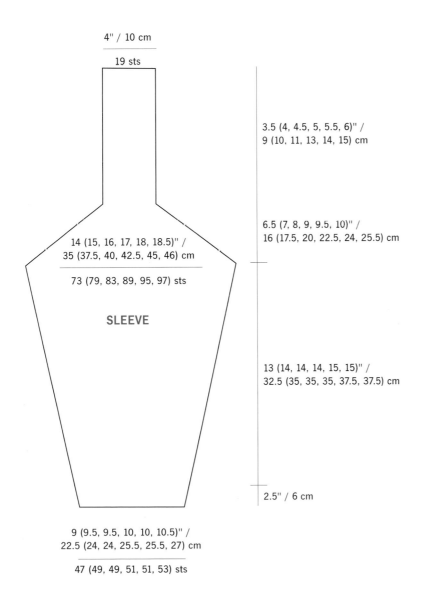

4" / 10 cm

19 sts

3.5 (4, 4.5, 5, 5.5, 6)" / 9 (10, 11, 13, 14, 15) cm

6.5 (7, 8, 9, 9.5, 10)" / 16 (17.5, 20, 22.5, 24, 25.5) cm

14 (15, 16, 17, 18, 18.5)" / 35 (37.5, 40, 42.5, 45, 46) cm

73 (79, 83, 89, 95, 97) sts

SLEEVE

13 (14, 14, 14, 15, 15)" / 32.5 (35, 35, 35, 37.5, 37.5) cm

2.5" / 6 cm

9 (9.5, 9.5, 10, 10, 10.5)" / 22.5 (24, 24, 25.5, 25.5, 27) cm

47 (49, 49, 51, 51, 53) sts

97) stitches. Tag edge stitches to mark beginning of sleeve cap.

Shape sleeve cap by decreasing 1 stitch each end of every 4th row 6 (6, 9, 11, 11, 12) times, then every 2nd row 21 (24, 23, 24, 27, 27) times, 19 stitches remain for sleeve strap. Tag edge stitches to mark beginning of strap. Continue in pattern, maintaining 2 plain knit stitches at each edge, until strap measures 3.5 (4, 4.5, 5, 5.5, 6)" / 9 (10, 11, 13, 14, 15) cm. Scrap off or bind off all 19 stitches.

Finishing

Do not block. Seam the shoulder straps to the back of the sweater first: Match the tags at the beginning of the back shoulders to the tags at the base of the shoulder straps and sew the seam, starting at the neck edge. Then match the tags at the beginning of the sleeve cap and the beginning of the armholes. Finish seaming to the armhole. Repeat for the front seams. Sew the sleeve and side seams.

Neckband: Beginning at the back right shoulder seam, pick up 27 (31, 33, 35, 39, 41) stitches from the back, 19 from the left shoulder strap, approximately 34 (35, 37, 39, 40, 42) stitches along the left front, 1 center stitch, 34 (35, 37, 39, 40, 42) stitches along the right front, and 19 from the right shoulder strap. Work the first of row k1p1 rib, reducing stitches across back neck by knitting 2 stitches together 3 (3, 3, 3, 5, 5) times evenly spaced. Work both shoulder straps by knitting 2 together, knit 1, (knit 2 together) 8 times. Reducing the shoulder strap will prevent the neckline from stretching. Tag the center stitch of the neckline V. Work rib for 1.5" (4 cm), mitering the center of the V-neckline (page 43). Bind off loosely. Work in all yarn tails. Wash the sweater and lay it flat to dry to set the stitches and shape the garment.

Keeping Track of Decreases

To keep track of two sets of decreases when shaping the sweater front, make a chart like the one at right for the size you are knitting. Use a row counter to keep track of the row numbers and refer to the chart for neckline and armhole decreases. This is the chart for size medium (M).

Numbers in bold refer to armhole shaping. Bracketed numbers refer to neckline shaping. Note that some numbers are both bold and bracketed, which indicates shaping at both the armholes and the neckline.

6	[30]	[50]	[74]
12	[34]	[54]	[78]
18	36	[58]	[82]
[22]	[38]	[62]	[84]
24	[42]	[66]	
[26]	[46]	[70]	

Mitering the Neckband

The center of this neckband is mitered to fit the V of the sweater neckline with double decreases. One stitch is decreased on each side of the center stitch at the same time, with the center stitch always riding on the front for a small, decorative detail.

The center stitch remains in front of the two decreased stitches.

Beginning with the second round and then every alternate round, work up to 1 stitch before the center stitch. Slip the next 2 stitches (the center stitch and the one before it) *together* as if to knit, as shown in drawing at right. This will place the center stitch on the right needle first.

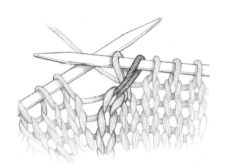

Slip the center stitch and the stitch before it together, as if to knit.

Then knit the first stitch after the center stitch and pass both slipped stitches over it as shown.

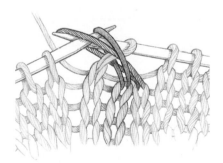

Knit the next stitch and then pass the two slipped stitches over it.

desert dreams

This collared cardigan, sized from X-small to XX-large, features a rich, seeded rib texture.

Featured Design Variations

• Raglan silhouette
• Ribbed collar and bands
• Seeded rib patterning

Yarn: Tahki Yarns "Shannon" 100% wool with 92 yards (85 meters) per 1.75 ounce (50 gram) ball, 13 (14, 17, 19, 22, 24) balls color #24

Needles: Size US 5 (3.75 mm), 6 (4 mm), and 7 (4.5 mm) OR SIZE TO OBTAIN GAUGE

Notions: tape measure, tapestry needle, 5 buttons: JHB "Modernity" (clear/nickel, #15446), ⅞" (2.5 cm)

Gauge: 20 stitches and 26 rows = 4" (10 cm) over seeded rib pattern on larger needles

Sizes: Women's XS (S, M, L, XL, XXL). Model is wearing size S.

Finished Measurements

Chest measurement: 36.5 (39.5, 44.5, 47.5, 52.5, 55.5)" / 93 (100, 113, 121, 133, 141) cm

Garment length: 24 (24.5, 26.5, 27.75, 29.5, 30)" / 61 (62, 67, 70, 75, 76) cm

Center back to cuff: 27.5 (28.75, 31.5, 33.25, 35.5, 36.75)" / 70 (73, 80, 84, 90, 93) cm

Notes:

(1) Begin all garment pieces with 1 knit stitch at right edge and end with 2 at the left to balance the pattern. (2) Always slip the first stitch and knit the last for perfect edges. (3) I like the way this particular yarn looks when it is washed in hot water because the fiber really "blooms" and fills out the stitches. Allow for that factor when you swatch. (4) Work all increases and decreases 2 stitches from the edge. (5) The k1p1 ribbed collar is worked on progressively larger needles for better shaping.

Back

With the smaller needle, cast on 91 (99, 111, 119, 131, 139) stitches and work k1p1 rib for 1" (2.5 cm). Change to larger needle and work seeded rib until piece measures 13 (13, 14, 14, 15, 15)" / 33 (33, 36, 36, 38, 38) cm from the cast-on edge. Tag the edge stitches to mark the beginning of the armholes.

Bind off 1 stitch at each end of the next row and the following 4th rows 4 (5, 7, 9, 9, 10) more times. Then bind off 1 stitch at each end of every alternate row 10 (10, 9, 8, 10, 10) times. 61 (67, 77, 83, 91, 97) stitches. When the armhole measures 6.5 (7, 8, 9, 9.5, 10)" / 17 (18, 20, 23, 24, 25) cm,

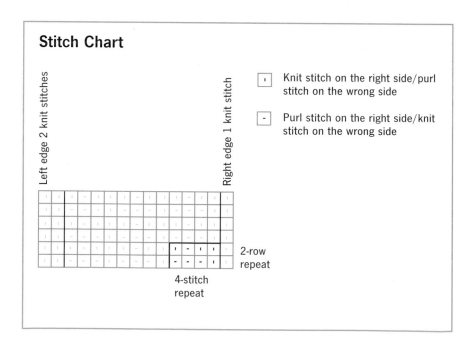

Stitch Chart

Left edge 2 knit stitches

Right edge 1 knit stitch

| · | Knit stitch on the right side/purl stitch on the wrong side |
| − | Purl stitch on the right side/knit stitch on the wrong side |

2-row repeat

4-stitch repeat

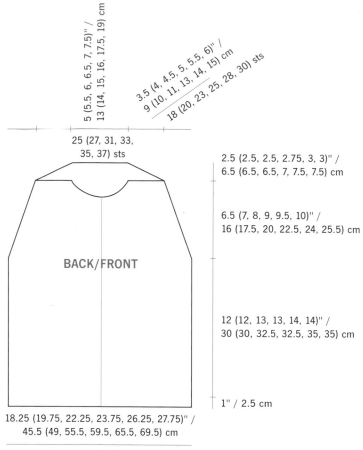

5 (5.5, 6, 6.5, 7, 7.5)" /
13 (14, 15, 16, 17.5, 19) cm

3.5 (4, 4.5, 5, 5.5, 6)" /
9 (10, 11, 13, 14, 15) cm

18 (20, 23, 25, 28, 30) sts

25 (27, 31, 33, 35, 37) sts

2.5 (2.5, 2.5, 2.75, 3, 3)" /
6.5 (6.5, 6.5, 7, 7.5, 7.5) cm

6.5 (7, 8, 9, 9.5, 10)" /
16 (17.5, 20, 22.5, 24, 25.5) cm

BACK/FRONT

12 (12, 13, 13, 14, 14)" /
30 (30, 32.5, 32.5, 35, 35) cm

1" / 2.5 cm

18.25 (19.75, 22.25, 23.75, 26.25, 27.75)" /
45.5 (49, 55.5, 59.5, 65.5, 69.5) cm

91 (99, 111, 119, 131, 139) sts

8.75 (9.5, 10.25, 11, 12.75, 13.5)" /
22 (24, 26, 27.5, 32, 34) cm

43 (47, 51, 55, 63, 67) sts

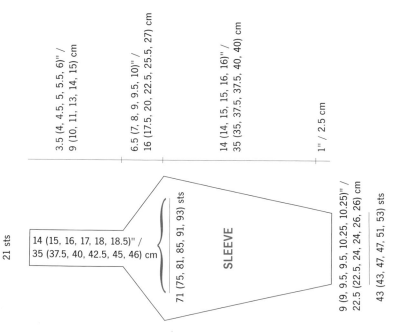

3.5 (4, 4.5, 5, 5.5, 6)" /
9 (10, 11, 13, 14, 15) cm

6.5 (7, 8, 9, 9.5, 10)" /
16 (17.5, 20, 22.5, 25.5, 27) cm

14 (14, 15, 15, 16, 16)" /
35 (35, 37.5, 37.5, 40, 40) cm

1" / 2.5 cm

4" / 10 cm

21 sts

14 (15, 16, 17, 18, 18.5)" /
35 (37.5, 40, 42.5, 45, 46) cm

71 (75, 81, 85, 91, 93) sts

SLEEVE

9 (9, 9.5, 9.5, 10.25, 10.25)" /
22.5 (22.5, 24, 24, 26, 26) cm

43 (43, 47, 47, 51, 53) sts

tag each edge stitch to mark the beginning of the shoulders.

Bind off 2 stitches at the beginning of the next 12 (8, 2, 4, 4, 0) rows then bind off 3 stitches at the beginning of the next 4 (8, 14, 14, 16, 20) rows. Scrap off/bind off the remaining 25 (27, 31, 33, 35, 37) back neck stitches.

Fronts

Knit two with reversed shaping. With the smaller needle, cast on 43 (47, 51, 55, 63, 67) stitches and work as for back until armhole measures ¾" (2 cm) less than back. Continue armhole decreases and *at the same time* shape neckline on opposite edge by binding off 5 (6, 6, 7, 7, 8) stitches once, 3 (3, 3, 3, 5, 6) stitches once, and 2 stitches once. Scrap off/bind off remaining 18 (20, 23, 25, 28, 30) shoulder stitches.

Sleeves

Knit two alike. With the smaller needle, cast on 43 (43, 47, 47, 51, 53) stitches and work k1p1 rib for 1" (2.5 cm). Change to the larger needle and work seeded rib pattern, *at the same time* increasing 1 stitch at each end of every 6th row 14 (13, 14, 9, 10, 10) times and every 4th row 0 (3, 3, 10, 10, 10) times, until piece measures 15 (15, 16, 16, 17, 17)" / 38 (38, 41, 41, 43, 43) cm from the cast-on edge and there are 71 (75, 81, 85, 91, 93) stitches. Tag the edge stitches to mark the beginning of the sleeve cap shaping.

Bind off 1 stitch at each end of every alternate row 17 (19, 22, 26, 27, 30) times then every row 8 (8, 8, 6, 8, 6) times. When cap measures 6.5 (7, 8, 9, 9.5, 10)" / 17 (18, 20, 23, 24, 25) cm and there are 21 stitches, tag the edge stitches to mark the beginning of the shoulder strap.

Work 3.5 (4, 4.5, 5, 5.5, 6)" / 9 (10, 11, 13, 14, 15) cm straight and then scrap off/bind off the 21 shoulder strap stitches.

Finishing

Lightly block all pieces. Using the edge tags to match sections, join the back shoulder seams to the back edges of the shoulder straps. Join front shoulder to shoulder straps. Complete all armhole seams. Sew sleeve and side seams.

Collar: With the right side of the garment facing you and with the smaller needle (US 5 [3.75 mm]), pick up 10 (11, 11, 12, 14, 16) stitches from the right front neck, 21 stitches from the right shoulder strap, 25 (27, 31, 33, 35, 37) back neck stitches, 21 stitches from the left shoulder strap, and 10 (11, 11, 12, 14, 16) stitches from the left front neck. Work k1p1 rib for 2" (5 cm). Work next 2" (5 cm) with US 6 (4 mm) needle and last 2" (5 cm) with US 7 (4.5 mm) needle. Bind off loosely.

Button band (left): With the right side of the garment facing you and with the smallest needle, pick up *approximately* 84 (87, 95, 100, 107, 109) stitches along the left front edge and 20 more stitches along the edge of the collar. Work k1p1 rib for 6 rows then bind off loosely.

Buttonhole band (right): Pick up as for the button band and work 6 rows rib, making 5 evenly spaced 2-stitch buttonholes in the 3rd row. The top buttonhole should be 2 to 3 stitches from the top edge and the bottom buttonhole about 1.5" (4 cm) from the bottom edge. Divide the remaining stitches to provide an equal number of stitches between each 2-stitch buttonhole.

Work in all tails. Sew the buttons to the left front. Wash the finished sweater and lay flat to dry.

Two-Row Buttonholes

Decide on the placement and spacing of the buttonholes and mark them with safety pins or stitch markers. This is easiest to do after you have knitted the first two rows of the band and can count the actual stitches.

On the third row of the band, work up to the first buttonhole placement. Knit the two buttonhole stitches (individually, not together) and then pass the first stitch over the second stitch. Knit the next stitch and pass the previous stitch over it. The two stitches you marked for the buttonhole should be bound off. Work up to each of the remaining buttonholes and repeat this step.

On the next (in this case, fourth) row of the buttonhole band, you need to cast on stitches to replace the ones you bound off in the previous row. Work up to each buttonhole and cast on 2 stitches using the simple looped cast-on method (page 90).

Stitches that are cast on with the simple looped method tend to shift and tighten irregularly. So, when you knit them in the next (fifth) row of the band, knit them through the back loop to stabilize them and produce a nicer edge for the buttonhole. This method does not affect a 2-stitch buttonhole much, but it does make a difference with larger buttonholes.

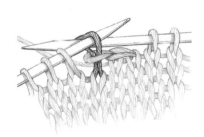

Row 3 of the band: Knit up to the buttonhole placement. Knit 2 stitches, then pass the first stitch over the second. Knit the next stitch and pass the previous stitch over it.

When the next row (the 4th row of the band) is knitted, use a simple looped cast-on method to cast on 2 stitches (page 90). When you knit these stitches in the next row, knitting them through the back loop will strengthen the buttonhole.

OK kids

Cables cover the surfaces of these sweaters, traveling right up the sleeves and into the neckband.

Featured Design Variations

• Raglan silhouette
• k2p2 rib bands
• 2×2 cables

Yarn: Nashua Handknit's "Julia" 25% alpaca, 25% mohair, 50% wool with 97 yards (88 meters) per ball, 7 (8, 9, 11, 12) balls color #NHJ2230 Rock Henna (for boy's sweater) or #NHJ5178 Lupine (for girl's sweater)

Needles: Size US 5 (3.75 mm) and 7 (4.5 mm) straight or circular needles and 16" (40 cm) circular for neckband size 5 (3.75 mm) OR SIZE TO OBTAIN GAUGE

Notions: tape measure, row counter, tapestry needle

Gauge: 24 stitches and 26 rows = 4" (10 cm) with cable pattern worked on size 7 (4.5 mm) needle

Sizes: Children's XS (S, M, L, XL). Boy is wearing size M and the girl is wearing size XL.

Finished Measurements

Chest measurement: 26 (28.5, 31, 33, 35.5)" / 66 (72, 79, 84, 90) cm

Garment length: 16 (17.5, 19, 21, 23)" / 41 (44, 48, 53, 58) cm

Center back to sleeve cuff: 20 (22.5, 24.5, 26, 27.5)" / 51 (57, 62, 66, 70) cm

Notes:

(1) Work all garment pieces with 1 knit stitch at each edge. This stitch should be slipped at the beginning and knitted through the back loop at the end of each row. The shoulder strap requires 2 knit stitches at each edge, reducing the purl stitches from 3 to 2 on each side of the cable. (2) End all ribs with a wrong-side row. Evenly increase stitches as required over the next row and also establish k4p3 placement of the pattern. (3) Because the neckline is shaped over so few rows, it is faster to knit one side of the neckline and then the other, rather than attaching a second ball of yarn to work both sides simultaneously. (4) Tag the stitches as instructed as matching the tags will make assembly simpler and more accurate.

Stitch Chart

Left edge stitch

Center 12 stitches for shoulder strap

Right edge stitch

| ı | Knit stitch on the right side/purl stitch on the wrong side |

| – | Purl stitch on the right side/knit stitch on the wrong side |

2x2 front cross cable: Remove 2 stitches on cable needle and hold to front. Knit 2 stitches from left needle and then 2 stitches from cable needle.

Back

With the smaller needle, cast on 74 (82, 90, 98, 102) stitches and work k2p2 rib (beginning and ending the row with k2) for 2" (5 cm), ending with a wrong-side row. Change to the larger needles and establish the pattern, *at the same time* evenly increasing 5 (4, 3, 2, 5) stitches across the row. 79 (86, 93, 100, 107) stitches. The cable pattern should begin k1 (edge stitch), p2 at the right edge, followed by 10 (11, 12, 13, 14) repeats of [k4, p3], and the row should end with k4, p1, k1 (edge stitch) at the left edge. This will guarantee 3 purl stitches coming together at the side seams when the front and back are joined. Work the cable pattern until the piece measures 9.5 (10, 11, 12, 14)" / 24 (25, 28, 30, 36) cm from the cast-on edge. Tag the edge stitches to mark the beginning of the armhole.

Shape the armholes at each side by decreasing 1 stitch at each end of the next and every 4th row 2 (5, 5, 6, 6) times, then every other row 11 (8, 10, 10, 11) times. 53 (60, 63, 68, 73) stitches remain. Tag the edge stitches to mark the beginning of the back shoulder slant. Bind off 2 stitches at the beginning of the next 0 (6, 6, 2, 4) rows, then 3 stitches at the beginning of the next 10 (8, 8, 12, 12). Scrap off/bind off the remaining 23 (24, 27, 28, 29) back neck stitches.

Front

Work same as back to the armhole shaping, *at the same time* begin shaping the front neck when 59 (66, 69, 74, 79) stitches remain. Work across 21 (24, 24, 26, 28) stitches. Bind off the next 17 (18, 21, 22, 23) stitches and work across the remaining 21 (24, 24, 26, 28) stitches. Working the right side of the

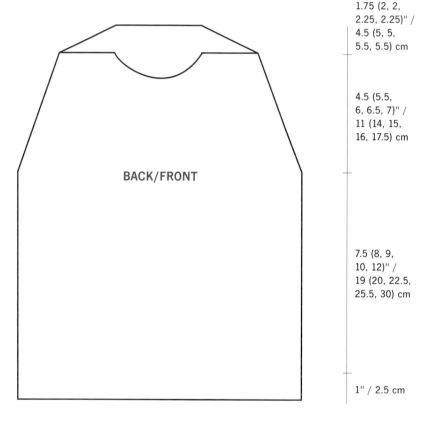

9 (10, 10.5, 11.25, 12)" / 22.5 (25.5, 27, 28, 30) cm

53 (60, 63, 68, 73) sts

4 (4, 4.5, 4.75, 5)" / 10 (10, 11, 12, 13) cm

23 (24, 27, 28, 29) sts

2.5 (3, 3.25, 3.25, 3.5)" / 6.5 (7.5, 8.5, 8.5, 9) cm

15 (18, 18, 20, 22) sts

1.75 (2, 2, 2.25, 2.25)" / 4.5 (5, 5, 5.5, 5.5) cm

4.5 (5.5, 6, 6.5, 7)" / 11 (14, 15, 16, 17.5) cm

BACK/FRONT

7.5 (8, 9, 10, 12)" / 19 (20, 22.5, 25.5, 30) cm

1" / 2.5 cm

13 (14.25, 15.5, 16.5, 17.75)" / 32.5 (35.5, 39, 41, 38) cm

79 (86, 93, 100, 107) sts

neckline only and continuing the arm-hole decreases, bind off 1 stitch every other row at the neck edge until 15 (18, 18, 20, 22) stitches remain. Bind off *loosely* or scrap off. Repeat the neckline shaping for the left side of the neckline.

Sleeves

With the smaller needles, cast on 34 (34, 42, 46, 46) stitches and work k2p2 (beginning and ending with k2) rib for 2" (5 cm). Change to the larger needles and evenly increase 2 (2, 0, 2, 2) stitches across the row. 36 (36, 42, 48, 48) stitches. Establish the cable pattern so that the 12-stitch repeat shown in the chart (page 48) is centered on the sleeve. For sizes X-small and small, k1, p1 (k4, p3) 4 times, end k4, p1, k1. For medium, k2 (p3, k4) 5 times, end p3, k2. For large and X-large, k5, (p3, k4) 5 times, end p3, k5. Work the cable pattern until the sleeve measures 11 (12, 13, 14, 15)" / 28 (30, 33, 36, 38) cm from the cast-on edge, *at the same time* increasing 1 stitch at each end of every 6th row 3 (0, 3, 6, 2) times, every 4th row 8 (13, 11, 8, 15) times, and every other row 0 (2, 0, 0, 0) times. 58 (66, 70, 76, 82) stitches. Tag the edge stitches to mark beginning of sleeve cap.

Shape the sleeve cap by decreasing 1 stitch at each end of every row 17 (19, 19, 23, 25) times, then every other row 6 (8, 10, 9, 10) times. 12 stitches remain for shoulder strap. Tag the edge stitches to mark the beginning of strap. The pattern for the strap becomes k2, p2, k4 (cable), p2, k2. Work the shoulder strap for 2.5 (3, 3.25, 3.25, 3.5)" / 6.5 (7.5, 8, 8, 9) cm. Scrap off or place all 12 stitches on a stitch holder. These stitches should not be bound off as they continue into the neckband.

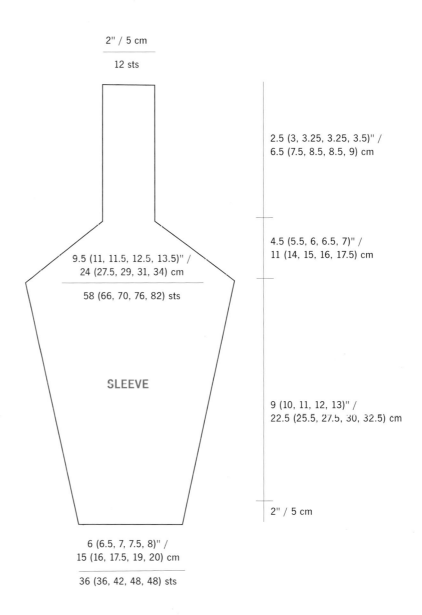

2" / 5 cm

12 sts

2.5 (3, 3.25, 3.25, 3.5)" / 6.5 (7.5, 8.5, 8.5, 9) cm

4.5 (5.5, 6, 6.5, 7)" / 11 (14, 15, 16, 17.5) cm

9.5 (11, 11.5, 12.5, 13.5)" / 24 (27.5, 29, 31, 34) cm

58 (66, 70, 76, 82) sts

SLEEVE

9 (10, 11, 12, 13)" / 22.5 (25.5, 27.5, 30, 32.5) cm

2" / 5 cm

6 (6.5, 7, 7.5, 8)" / 15 (16, 17.5, 19, 20) cm

36 (36, 42, 48, 48) sts

Finishing

Do not block garment pieces. Use the tags to match the back shoulders and back edges of the shoulder straps and sew both seams. Use the tags to match the front shoulders and front edges of shoulder straps and sew both seams. Sew all four armhole seams, using tags to match the beginning edges of armholes and the sleeve caps. Sew the side and sleeve seams.

Neckband: With the smaller needle and beginning at the right back shoulder seam, pick up back neck stitches and make 1 (0, 1, 0, 0) for 24 (24, 28, 28, 28) back neck stitches, 12 shoulder strap stitches, 28 (28, 32, 32, 32) front neck stitches, and 12 shoulder strap stitches. Set up the k2p2 rib pattern across the back, knitting 2 together twice evenly spaced to end with k2 at the left back seam. When working the last knit stitch on the back, knit it together with the first shoulder strap stitch. Work (k1, p2, k4, p2, k1) across left shoulder stitches (to continue the cable pattern established on the shoulder strap) and work the last shoulder stitch together with the first left front neck stitch (k2 together).

Continue the k2p2 pattern across the front neck stitches, knitting 2 together twice evenly spaced so that pattern continues correctly into the shoulder strap. Work the last right front neck stitch together with the first right shoulder strap stitch as k2 together. Continue the cable pattern across the right shoulder strap, knitting the last stitch together with the first k1 of the back. The rib should continue around the neckband as k2p2, broken only by the shoulder strap cables that flow seamlessly into the neckband. Work the neckband for 1.5" (4 cm), crossing the cables in the sequence established, and then bind off loosely.

The center sleeve cable continues through the shoulder strap and into the neckband.

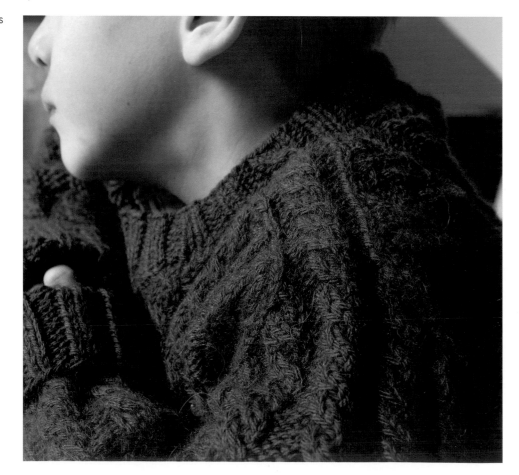

Knitting Cables

Cables come in many sizes and combinations. From tiny 1x1 to enormous 5x5 cables, most are easily described by the number of stitches that cross each other and the direction and the order in which they cross. Basic cables usually feature groups of knit stitches crossing knit stitches, but many cables also include purl stitches in one group or the other and often in between them. For those cables, the knit and purl symbols are clearly shown in the chart and usually explained more fully in the code for the chart.

Generally, when knitters talk about a front cross or back cross cable, they are referring to the location of the cable needle and, ultimately, the stitches it holds. For example, if you place two stitches on a cable needle and hold the cable needle behind the work, you will knit a back cross cable. Hold the cable needle at front and it is called a front cross cable. The stitches on the front of the cable will slant either left or right as a result of the placement of the cable needle, so these cables are sometimes called left cross and right cross cables. When cables are described as 2x2 or 3 over 1, the first number indicates how many stitches are visible on the face of the cable and how many cross behind it.

Rather than refer to the cable by name, patterns usually just show the symbols in a chart and give a code that explains the chart. I find that as I work a cable, I think in terms of "so many stitches to the front" in relation to how the stitches appear on the chart. If you really understand what is in front and which direction the stitches should cross, you will make far fewer mistakes than you would if you just blindly follow the directions. When you begin to combine cables for larger effects, it is essential that the right number of stitches cross in the correct direction.

OK Kids calls for a 2x2 front cross cable, but there is no reason not to knit a back cross cable if you prefer. You could also knit 1x3 or 3x1 cables as shown in the chart, although there's a chance that your sweater would actually knit up a little larger. Those types of cables tend to be a somewhat more relaxed and draw the fabric in less than their 2x2 cousins.

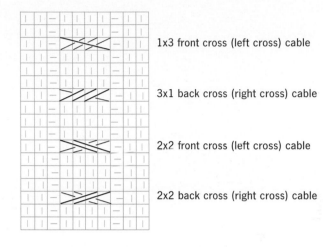

1x3 front cross (left cross) cable

3x1 back cross (right cross) cable

2x2 front cross (left cross) cable

2x2 back cross (right cross) cable

To knit a 1x3 front cross/left cross cable:
Remove 1 stitch on a cable needle and hold it in front of the work. Knit the next 3 stitches from the left needle and then knit the stitch on the cable needle. The single stitch on the right side of the fabric will slant from right to left.

To knit a 3x1 back cross/right cross cable:
Remove 1 stitch on a cable needle and hold it behind the work. Knit the next 3 stitches from the left needle and then the stitch on the cable needle. Three stitches on the right side of the fabric will slant from left to right.

To knit a 2x2 front cross/left cross cable:
Remove the first 2 stitches on a cable needle and hold in front of the work. Knit 2 stitches from the left needle and then the 2 stitches on the cable needle. The stitches on the right side of the fabric will slant from right to left.

To knit a 2x2 back cross/right cross cable:
Remove the first 2 stitches on a cable needle and hold behind the work. Knit 2 stitches from the left needle and then the 2 stitches on the cable needle. The stitches on the right side of the fabric will slant from left to right.

blue bonnets

Although this is not a traditional saddle-shouldered garment, this little tank top features a raised twisted-stitch variation and back-dropped shoulder seams for a smooth silhouette.

Featured Design Variations

- Sleeveless silhouette
- Quick and easy edge finishes

Yarn: Cascade Yarns "Sierra" 80% pima cotton, 20% merino wool with 191 yards (174 meters) per 3.5 ounce (100 gram) skein, 3 (4, 4, 5, 5) skeins color #27

Needles: Size US 7 (4.5 mm) straight or circular needles for body and 16" (41 cm) circular for edgings OR SIZE TO OBTAIN GAUGE

Notions: tape measure, tapestry needle

Gauge: 18 stitches and 29 rows = 4" (10 cm) worked in pattern stitch

Sizes: Women's S (M, L, XL, XXL). Model is wearing size S.

Finished Measurements

Chest measurement: 35.5 (40, 44.5, 49, 53)" / 90 (102, 113, 125, 135) cm

Garment length: 21 (23, 24, 24.75, 26)" / 53 (59, 61, 63, 65) cm

Shoulders: 12 (13.5, 14.5, 15.5, 16)" / 30 (34, 37, 39, 41) cm

Notes:

(1) The swatch should be washed and dried exactly as you plan to treat your finished sweater. The swatch and the model garment were hand washed, spun damp in the washing machine, laid flat to partially dry, and then finished in the dryer. (2) Always slip the first stitch and knit the last stitch in every row.

Stitch Chart

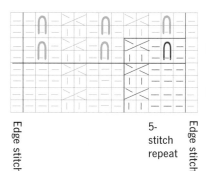

2-row pattern repeat

Rib

Edge stitch

5-stitch repeat

Edge stitch

First row and all odd-numbered rows are wrong-side rows.

| Knit stitch on the right side/purl stitch on the wrong side

— Purl stitch on the right side/knit stitch on the wrong side

Twisted stitch (worked on right-side rows): Insert right needle through second stitch on left needle and knit, leaving stitch on left needle. Knit first stitch from left needle and then release both stitches.

Tuck stitch: Purl stitch on right-side rows. On wrong-side rows, insert right needle to knit into center of stitch one row below stitch on left needle.

2.5 (3.25, 3.75, 4.25, 4.25)" /
6.5 (8.5, 9.5, 10.5, 10.5) cm
12 (15, 17, 19, 19) sts

6.5 (6.5, 7, 7, 7.5)" /
16 (16, 17.5, 17.5, 19) cm
30 (30, 32, 32, 34) sts

End back here.

BACK/FRONT

0.75" / 2 cm

3" / 7.5 cm

1" / 2.5 cm

5.5 (6.5,
7, 7.25, 7.5)" /
14 (16, 17.5,
18, 19) cm

13 (14, 14.5,
15, 16)" /
32.5 (35, 36,
37.5, 40) cm

17.75 (20, 22.25, 24.5, 26.5)" / 44.5 (50, 55.5, 61, 66) cm

80 (90, 100, 110, 120) sts

Back

Cast on 80 (90, 100, 110, 120) stitches and work rib pattern for 1" (2.5 cm). Continue with main pattern until work measures 13 (14, 14.5, 15, 16)" / 33 (36, 37, 38, 41) cm from cast-on edge. Shape armholes by binding off at the beginning of each row 5 stitches twice, 4 stitches 0 (2, 2, 2, 2) times, 3 stitches twice, 2 stitches 2 (2, 2, 4, 6) times, and 1 stitch 6 (2, 6, 8, 12) times.

Work even until the back measures 5.5 (6.5, 7, 7.25, 7.5)" / 14 (17, 18, 18, 19) cm from the beginning of the armhole. Separately bind off or scrap off 12 (15, 17, 19, 19) stitches for each shoulder and 30 (30, 32, 32, 34) stitches for the back neck.

Front

Work the same as for back until piece measures 6.5 (7.5, 8, 8.25, 8.5)" / 17 (19, 20, 21, 22) cm from the beginning of the armhole to begin shaping the front neck.

Work 18 (21, 23, 25, 26) stitches. Attach a second ball of yarn, bind off the center 18 (18, 20, 20, 20) stitches and work to the end of the row. Working both sides of the neck at the same time (or separately if you prefer), bind off at each neck edge on alternate rows 3 stitches once, 2 stitches once, and 1 stitch 1 (1, 1, 1, 2) times. Work straight on the remaining 12 (15, 17, 19, 19) stitches until each shoulder measures 3" (7 cm) from the beginning of the neck shaping.

To shape the shoulders, at each armhole edge on alternate rows, bind off 4 (5, 6, 7, 7) stitches 3 (3, 2, 1, 1) times, then 0 (0, 5, 6, 6) stitches 0 (0, 1, 2, 2) times. If you worked short rows at the end of each row, instead of binding off, scrap off all 12 (15, 17, 19, 19) stitches.

Twisted Stitch Variation

Although this is a twisted stitch pattern, it is executed a little differently. Usually, a twisted stitch is worked by passing the right needle through just the right/front leg of the second stitch in *front of the first stitch*, rather than through it, as shown in the Glossary, page 90.

To make this twisted stitch variation, when the right needle is inserted into the second stitch on the left needle, it passes *straight through the stitch* to the back, where the yarn is wrapped around the needle. Then the first stitch is knitted and both stitches are dropped from the left needle together. This modification creates a dramatic, raised effect. If you prefer, you can substitute a regular twisted stitch. Your sweater would also have a little more ease.

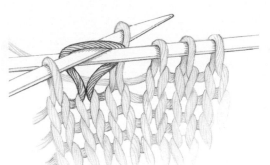

When knitting this variation of a twisted stitch, the right needle is inserted through the second stitch on the left needle to knit it. Then the first stitch is knitted and both stitches released from the left needle.

The resulting texture is more raised than it would be if the stitches were conventionally twisted.

Finishing

Working one full stitch from the edge, sew the side seams. With the right side of the garment facing you, beginning at the side seam and working 1 full stitch from the edge, pick up approximately 64 (70, 74, 78, 82) stitches around the armhole edge. Purl 1 row and bind off loosely. Repeat for the second armhole. For neckline, with right side facing you and beginning at back right, pick up 30 (30, 32, 32, 34) stitches across the back neck, 14 stitches along side, 30 (30, 32, 32, 34) from front, and 14 stitches along second side. Purl 1 row and bind off. Wash and dry the finished garment.

The simple one-row edging complements the twisted-stitch patterning.

rodeo

A simple one-by-one color pattern, mixed with an occasional row of garter stitch, produces a color effect that looks more complex than it is.

Featured Design Variations

- Modified drop-shoulder silhouette
- One-by-one color work
- Garter stitch

Yarn: Debbie Bliss "Cashmerino Aran" 55% merino wool, 33% microfiber, 12% cashmere with 98 yards (90 meters) per 1.75 ounce (50 gram) ball, 3 (4, 4, 5, 5, 6) balls each #502 (green/CC1), #014 (plum/CC2), #007 (rust/CC3), and 4 (4, 5, 5, 6, 7) balls #004 (navy/MC)

Needles: Size US 8 (5 mm) and 6 (4 mm) straight or circular and 16" (40 cm) circular US 6 (4 mm) for neckband OR SIZE TO OBTAIN GAUGE

Notions: tape measure, yellow highlighter, tapestry needle

Gauge: 20 stitches and 25 rows = 4" (10 cm) worked over pattern on larger needles

Sizes: Women's sizes XS (S, M, L, XL, XXL). Model is wearing size M.

Finished Measurements

Chest measurement: 36 (40, 44, 48, 52, 56)" / 91 (102, 112, 122, 132, 142) cm

Garment length: 21.5 (22, 23.5, 25, 26.5, 28)" / 55 (57, 60, 64, 67, 71) cm

Center back to cuff: 29 (30, 31, 32, 33, 34)" / 74 (76, 79, 81, 84, 86) cm

Notes:

(1) Always maintain 1 plain knit stitch at each edge, slipping the first stitch in the row and knitting the last. Work all increases inside this stitch. (2) The stitch chart represents the right side of the fabric, beginning with a wrong-side row. (3) The pattern is a 2-stitch/16-row repeat with each color knitting 6 rows in rotation (2 rows with the previous color, 2 rows alone, and 2 with the next color). Every 4th row is worked as reverse stockinette to produce the surface ridges in the pattern. (4) The two-color work is easiest and fastest to do if you can hold one yarn in your right hand (American style) and the other in your left (European style). (5) Cut the yarn at the end of each section and either work the ends in as you knit or work them into the seams later on. (6) Always make a note of the ending pattern row and the colors used to bind off to make sure that edges match.

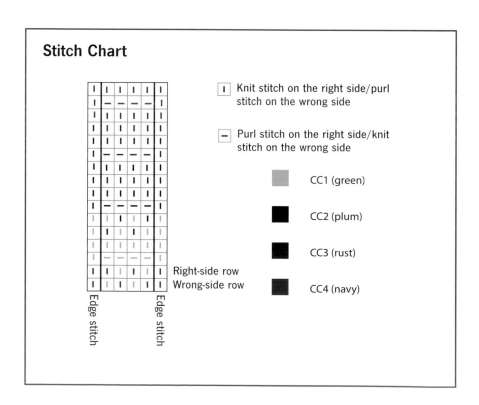

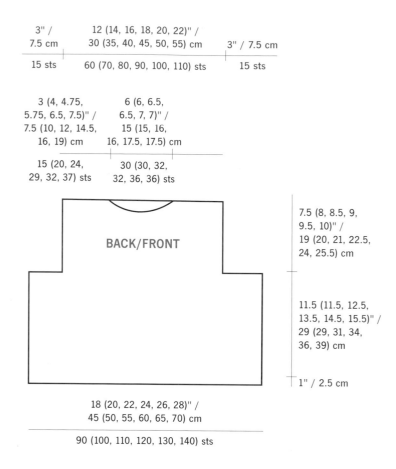

3" /
7.5 cm

12 (14, 16, 18, 20, 22)" /
30 (35, 40, 45, 50, 55) cm

3" / 7.5 cm

15 sts   60 (70, 80, 90, 100, 110) sts   15 sts

3 (4, 4.75,
5.75, 6.5, 7.5)" /
7.5 (10, 12, 14.5,
16, 19) cm

6 (6, 6.5,
6.5, 7, 7)" /
15 (15, 16,
16, 17.5, 17.5) cm

15 (20, 24,
29, 32, 37) sts

30 (30, 32,
32, 36, 36) sts

BACK/FRONT

7.5 (8, 8.5, 9,
9.5, 10)" /
19 (20, 21, 22.5,
24, 25.5) cm

11.5 (11.5, 12.5,
13.5, 14.5, 15.5)" /
29 (29, 31, 34,
36, 39) cm

1" / 2.5 cm

18 (20, 22, 24, 26, 28)" /
45 (50, 55, 60, 65, 70) cm

90 (100, 110, 120, 130, 140) sts

The pattern of small dots is formed by color changes in the garter-stitch sequence.

Back

With the smaller needle and the MC, cast on 90 (100, 110, 120, 130, 140) stitches and work 1" (2.5 cm) garter stitch. Change to the larger needles and, following the pattern chart, work 2 rows with MC and CC1, then two rows with CC1 alone. Continue following the chart until the piece measures 12.5 (12.5, 13.5, 14.5, 15.5, 16.5)" / 32 (32, 34, 37, 39, 42) cm from the cast-on edge. At the beginning of the next two rows, bind off 15 stitches to begin armhole. 60 (70, 80, 90, 100, 110) stitches remain. Work these stitches straight for 7.5 (8, 8.5, 9, 9.5, 10)" / 19 (20, 22, 23, 24, 25) cm. Scrap off/bind off 15 (20, 24, 29, 32, 37) stitches at each end for back shoulders and bind off the center 30 (30, 32, 32, 36, 36) stitches for the back neck.

Front

Work the front the same as the back until the armhole is 0.75" (2 cm) less than the back. Shape the neck by working across 18 (23, 27, 32, 35, 40) stitches, then binding off the center 24 (24, 26, 26, 30, 30) stitches. Work to the end of the row and then continue working one side of the neckline, binding off on alternate rows at the neck edge 2 stitches once and 1 stitch once. Scrap off the remaining 15 (20, 24, 29, 32, 37) stitches. Reattach the yarn to continue working the second side of the neckline to match the first.

Sleeves

Knit two alike. With the smaller needle and the MC, cast on 44 (46, 46, 48, 48, 50) stitches and work 1" (2.5 cm) of garter stitch. Change to the larger needles and follow pattern chart as for front/back, *at the same time* increasing 1 stitch at each end of every 6th row 8 (6, 1, 0, 0, 0) times, every 4th row 16 (19, 27, 29, 25, 24) times, and every 2nd row 0 (0, 0, 0, 7, 9) times. 92 (96,

102, 106, 112, 116) stitches. When sleeve measures 20" (51 cm) from the cast-on edge, tag the edge stitches to mark the beginning of the sleeve "cap" and work 3" (8 cm) straight.

At the beginning of the next 2 rows, bind off 38 (40, 43, 45, 48, 50) stitches. Work 3 (4, 4.75, 5.75, 6.5, 7.5)" / 8 (10, 12, 15, 17, 19) cm straight and then bind off the 16 shoulder strap stitches.

Finishing

Lightly block all pieces. Join the back shoulder stitches to the back edges of the shoulder straps, then join the front shoulders to the front edges. Sew the top of the sleeve to the armhole edges of the garment and the top 3" (8 cm) of the sleeve to the bound-off edges at the beginning of the armhole. Sew the sleeve seams and then the side seams, beginning 4" (10 cm) from the lower edge to allow for side vents. Work in all tails.

Vents: Beginning at the lower edge, with the right side of the garment facing you and the smaller needle with MC, pick up approximately 15 stitches from each edge and one stitch in the center. Knit 1" (2.5 cm) of garter stitch, working a double decrease over center 3 stitches on right-side rows as follows: slip 2 together (the center stitch and the one before it) as if to knit, knit the next stitch, then pass the 2 slipped stitches over. Bind off loosely.

Neckband: Begin at the right back shoulder seam with the right side of the garment facing you. With the shorter needle and the MC, pick up 24 (24, 26, 26, 30, 30) stitches across the back, 12 stitches from the left shoulder strap, 24 (24, 26, 26, 30, 30) from the front, and 12 from the right shoulder strap. Work 1" (2.5 cm) of garter stitch and bind off loosely.

Work in all tails. Wash the finished garment and lay flat to dry.

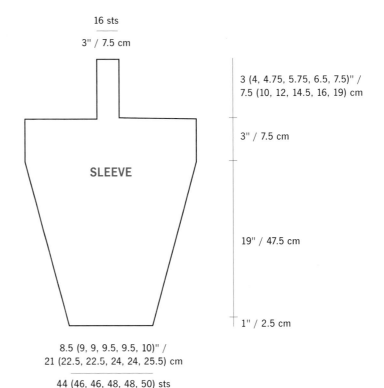

18.5 (19.25, 20.5, 21.25, 22.5, 23.25)" / 46 (48, 51, 53, 56, 58) cm

92 (96, 102, 106, 112, 116) sts

16 sts

3" / 7.5 cm

3 (4, 4.75, 5.75, 6.5, 7.5)" / 7.5 (10, 12, 14.5, 16, 19) cm

3" / 7.5 cm

SLEEVE

19" / 47.5 cm

1" / 2.5 cm

8.5 (9, 9, 9.5, 9.5, 10)" / 21 (22.5, 22.5, 24, 24, 25.5) cm

44 (46, 46, 48, 48, 50) sts

prairie

This feminine pullover is sized for both girls and women. The surface texture can easily be varied by working different cables or plain ribbing. The child's sweater was knit by machine (page 88).

Featured Design Variations

- Set-in sleeve silhouette
- Deep twisted stitch ribbings
- Funnel neckline

Yarn: Berroco "Pure Merino" 100% extra fine merino wool with 98 yards (85 meters) per 1.75 ounce (50 gram) ball, 4 (4, 5, 6, 7) balls color #8512, "Ballerina" for girls' sweater and 9 (11, 13, 14, 16) balls color #8571, "Sandstorm" for the women's.

Needles: Size US 7 (4.5 mm) and 9 (4.5 mm) straight or circular needles and 7 (4.5 mm) 16" (40 cm) circular needle OR SIZE TO OBTAIN GAUGE

Notions: tape measure, tapestry needle, yellow highlighter

Gauge: 18 stitches and 25 rows = 4" (10 cm) worked in stockinette on larger needles

Sizes: Girls' 4 (6, 8, 10, 12). Model is wearing size 12.

Women's S (M, L, XL, XXL). Model is wearing size M.

Girls' Finished Measurements

Chest measurement: 24 (25, 26, 28, 30)" / 61 (64, 66, 71, 76) cm

Garment length: 12 (13.25, 15, 16.5, 18.5)" / 30 (34, 38, 42, 47) cm

Center back to cuff: 18.75 (19.75, 20.5, 22, 24)" / 48 (50. 52. 56. 61) cm

Women's Finished Measurements

Chest measurement: 36 (40, 44, 48, 52)" / 91 (102, 112, 122, 132) cm

Garment length: 21 (22.75, 23.5, 24.25, 25.75)" / 53 (58, 60, 62, 65) cm

Center back to cuff: 26.75 (28, 30, 31.25, 32.5)" / 68 (71, 76, 79, 83) cm

Notes:

(1) All right-side rib rows begin slip 1, purl 1, twist 2, and end twist 2, purl 1, knit 1. This allows 1 seam stitch and ensures that 2 purls come together at the seams. It will also center the rib pattern on the sleeve cuff so that it continues correctly through sleeve, strap, and neckband. (2) The body of the garment is knitted in stockinette. (3) Directions are given for girls' sizes first, followed by women's sizes in brackets. Because these are long sequences of numbers, you should read through the entire pattern first and use a marker to highlight the numbers that refer to the size you are knitting. (4) To make sure the shoulder strap pattern continues smoothly into the neckband, scrap off the shoulder strap stitches or place them on a holder rather than binding them off.

Back

With the smaller needles, cast on 54 (58, 62, 66, 70) [82, 90, 98, 110, 118] stitches. Work twisted stitch rib as shown in the chart for 3" (8 cm) [4.5" (11 cm)]. Change to large needles and work stockinette for 3.5 (4.5, 6, 7, 8.5)" [7.5 (8.5, 9, 9.5, 10.5)"] / 9 (11, 15, 18, 22) cm [19 (22, 23, 24, 27) cm].

Shape the armholes by binding off at the beginning of the following rows 3 stitches twice, 2 stitches twice, 1 stitch 2 (4, 6, 6, 6) times for the girls' sweater *or* 5 stitches twice, 3 stitches 0 (2, 2, 2, 2) times, 2 stitches 2 (2, 2, 2, 4) times, and 1

Stitch Chart

2-row repeat

4-stitch repeat

 Twisted stitch: Knit second stitch on left needle, then knit first stitch. Release both stitches from left needle.

⊡ Knit stitch on the right side/purl stitch on the wrong side

⊟ Purl stitch on the right side/knit stitch on the wrong side

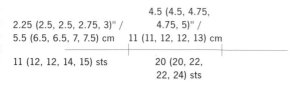

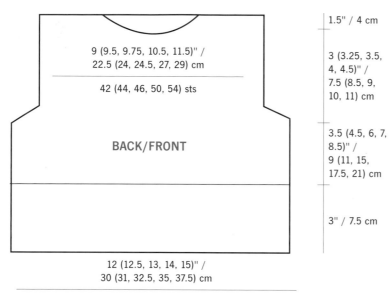

4.5 (4.5, 4.75, 4.75, 5)" /
11 (11, 12, 12, 13) cm

2.25 (2.5, 2.5, 2.75, 3)" /
5.5 (6.5, 6.5, 7, 7.5) cm

11 (12, 12, 14, 15) sts

20 (20, 22, 22, 24) sts

1.5" / 4 cm

9 (9.5, 9.75, 10.5, 11.5)" /
22.5 (24, 24.5, 27, 29) cm

42 (44, 46, 50, 54) sts

3 (3.25, 3.5, 4, 4.5)" /
7.5 (8.5, 9, 10, 11) cm

BACK/FRONT

3.5 (4.5, 6, 7, 8.5)" /
9 (11, 15, 17.5, 21) cm

3" / 7.5 cm

12 (12.5, 13, 14, 15)" /
30 (31, 32.5, 35, 37.5) cm

54 (58, 62, 66, 70) sts

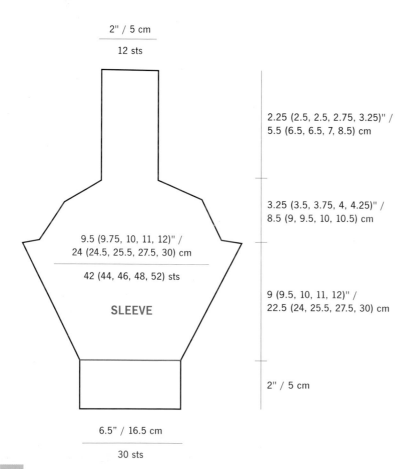

2" / 5 cm

12 sts

2.25 (2.5, 2.5, 2.75, 3.25)" /
5.5 (6.5, 6.5, 7, 8.5) cm

3.25 (3.5, 3.75, 4, 4.25)" /
8.5 (9, 9.5, 10, 10.5) cm

9.5 (9.75, 10, 11, 12)" /
24 (24.5, 25.5, 27.5, 30) cm

42 (44, 46, 48, 52) sts

9 (9.5, 10, 11, 12)" /
22.5 (24, 25.5, 27.5, 30) cm

SLEEVE

2" / 5 cm

6.5" / 16.5 cm

30 sts

stitch 10 (10, 10, 12, 12) times for the women's sweater. 42 (44, 46, 50, 54) [58 (60, 68, 74, 82)] stitches remain.

Work straight until the armhole measures 4.5 (4.75, 5, 5.5, 6)" [7.5 (8.25, 8.5, 8.75, 9.25)"] / 11 (12, 13, 14, 15) cm [19 (21, 22, 22, 23) cm]. Separately scrap off/bind off 11 (12, 12, 14, 15) [14 (15, 18, 20, 24)] stitches for each shoulder and 20 (20, 22, 22, 24) [30 (30, 32, 34, 34] stitches for the back neck.

Front

Work same as back until armhole measures 3 (3.25, 3.5, 4, 4.5)" [6 (6.75, 7, 7.25, 7.75)"] / 7 (8, 9, 10, 11) cm [15 (17, 18, 19, 20) cm].

Shape neckline as follows: Work across 16 (17, 17, 19, 20) [18 (19, 22, 24, 28)] stitches. Attach a second ball of yarn and bind off the center 10 (10, 12, 12, 14) [22 (22, 24, 26, 26)] stitches and work the remaining 16 (17, 17, 19, 20) [18 (19, 22, 24, 28)] stitches to the end of the row. Working both sides at the same time, decrease 1 stitch at neck edge every other row 5 [4] times. Scrap off/bind off the remaining sets of 11 (12, 12, 14, 15) [14 (15, 18, 20, 24)] shoulder stitches.

Sleeves

Knit two alike. With the smaller needles, cast on 30 [38 (38, 46, 46, 46)] stitches and work twisted stitch rib pattern for 2 [3]" (5 [8] cm) (page 92). Change to the larger needles and continue to work the center 12 [14] stitches in twisted-stitch rib pattern while working the remainder of the sleeve stitches in stockinette. *At the same time* increase 1 stitch at each end of every 8th row 6 (7, 5, 6, 3) times, then, every 6th row 0 (0, 3, 3, 8) times, [every 6th row 7 (3, 10, 5, 3) times, and every 4th row 7 (14, 5, 13, 17) times]. 42 (44, 46, 48, 52) [66 (72, 76, 82, 86)] stitches.

When sleeve measures 11 (11.5, 12, 13, 14)" [15.25 (15.75, 16.5, 17, 17.5)"]

/ 28 (29, 30, 33, 36) cm [39 (40, 42, 43, 44) cm] from cast-on edge, shape sleeve cap as follows:

For girls' sizes: At the beginning of the following rows, bind off 3 stitches twice, 2 stitches twice; 1 stitch 14 (16, 18, 20, 20) times, 2 stitches 0 (0, 0, 0, 2) times, and 3 stitches twice. 12 (patterned rib) stitches remain for shoulder strap.

For women's sizes: At the beginning of the following rows, bind off 5 stitches twice, 3 stitches 0 (2, 2, 2, 2) times, 2 stitches 2 (2, 2, 2, 4) times, 1 stitch 16 (16, 14, 16, 16) times, 2 stitches 4 (4, 4, 2, 2) times, 3 stitches 2 (2, 4, 4, 4) times, and 4 stitches 2 (2, 2, 4, 4) times. 14 (patterned rib) stitches remain for shoulder strap.

Work twisted-rib shoulder straps for 2.25 (2.5, 2.5, 2.75, 3.25)" [3.25 (3.5, 4.25, 4.75, 5)"] / 5 (6, 6, 7, 8) cm [8 (9, 11, 12, 13) cm], then scrap off or place on a stitch holder. Do not bind off these stitches.

Finishing
Lightly block all pieces. Join back shoulders to edges of shoulder straps. Then join front shoulders to front edges of shoulder straps. Sew the sleeve cap seams, then the sleeve and side seams.

Neckband: Starting at the right back shoulder seam, using the 16" (40 cm) circular needle, pick up (or return from holders or scrap knitting) 20 (20, 22, 22, 24) [30 (30, 32, 34, 34)] stitches from the back neck, 12 [14] from the left shoulder strap, 20 (20, 22, 22, 24) / 30 [30, 32, 34, 34)] stitches from the front neck, and 12 [14] stitches from the right shoulder strap. Neckband is worked in twisted-stitch rib pattern, which continues into neckband from each of the shoulder straps. In order to accommodate the pattern between them, it will be necessary to double 0 (0, 2, 2, 0) [0 (0, 2, 0, 0)] stitches on the back and front necks in the first row. Work twisted-stitch rib for 1.5 [3]" (4 [8] cm) and bind off loosely. Work in all tails.

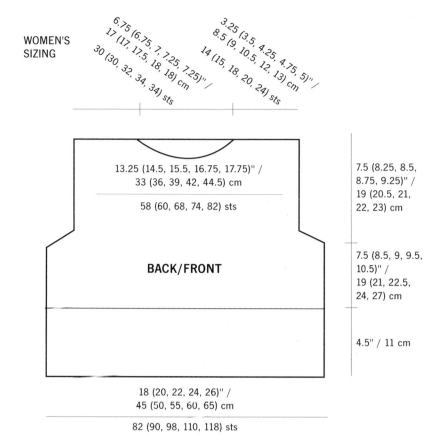

WOMEN'S SIZING

6.75 (6.75, 7, 7.25, 7.25)" / 17 (17, 17.5, 18, 18) cm
30 (30, 32, 34, 34) sts

3.25 (3.5, 4.25, 4.75, 5)" / 8.5 (9, 10.5, 12, 13) cm
14 (15, 18, 20, 24) sts

13.25 (14.5, 15.5, 16.75, 17.75)" / 33 (36, 39, 42, 44.5) cm
58 (60, 68, 74, 82) sts

BACK/FRONT

7.5 (8.25, 8.5, 8.75, 9.25)" / 19 (20.5, 21, 22, 23) cm

7.5 (8.5, 9, 9.5, 10.5)" / 19 (21, 22.5, 24, 27) cm

4.5" / 11 cm

18 (20, 22, 24, 26)" / 45 (50, 55, 60, 65) cm
82 (90, 98, 110, 118) sts

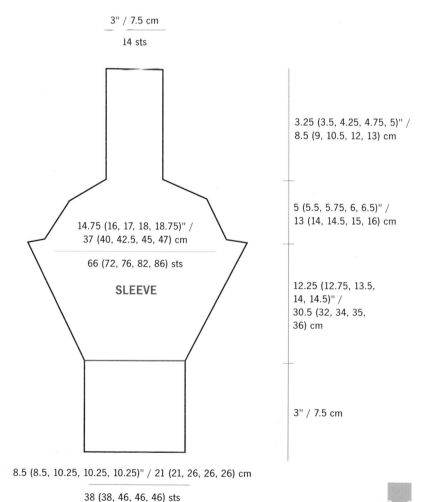

3" / 7.5 cm
14 sts

14.75 (16, 17, 18, 18.75)" / 37 (40, 42.5, 45, 47) cm
66 (72, 76, 82, 86) sts

SLEEVE

3.25 (3.5, 4.25, 4.75, 5)" / 8.5 (9, 10.5, 12, 13) cm

5 (5.5, 5.75, 6, 6.5)" / 13 (14, 14.5, 15, 16) cm

12.25 (12.75, 13.5, 14, 14.5)" / 30.5 (32, 34, 35, 36) cm

3" / 7.5 cm

8.5 (8.5, 10.25, 10.25, 10.25)" / 21 (21, 26, 26, 26) cm
38 (38, 46, 46, 46) sts

square dance

A simple, repeating pattern of knit and purl stitches creates this classic basket-weave pattern. The textured blocks catch light and shadow, adding dimension to the surface of this comfortable sweater.

Featured Design Variations

- Drop-shoulder silhouette
- Crew neck
- Garter-stitch bands

Yarn: Schuler "Schulana Alpacino" 54% virgin wool, 18% baby alpaca, 28% acrylic with 98 yards (90 meter) per 1.75 ounce (50 gram) ball, color #6, 10 (12, 13, 15, 17) balls

Needles: Size US 8 (5 mm) 24" (60 cm) circular and US 10 (6 mm) straight or circular needles OR SIZE TO OBTAIN GAUGE

Notions: tapestry needle, tape measure

Gauge: 16 stitches and 22 rows = 4" (10 cm) in basket-weave pattern

Sizes: XS (S, M, L, XL). Model is wearing size XS.

Finished Measurements

Chest measurement: 38 (43, 48, 53, 58)" / 97 (109, 122, 135, 147) cm

Garment Length: 23.5 (24, 24, 24.5, 25)" / 60 (61, 61, 62, 64) cm

Center back to sleeve cuff: 30 (31.25, 32.5, 33.75, 35" / 76 (79, 83, 86, 89) cm

Notes: (1) The featured yarn is subtly shaded and may stripe. To minimize this effect, work off two balls simultaneously, alternately knitting two rows with each. (2) Maintain 1 plain knit stitch at each edge of the front and back pieces and two at each edge of sleeve and shoulder strap.

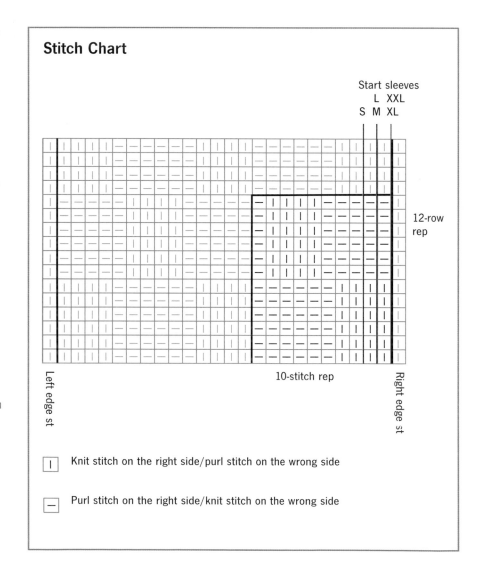

Stitch Chart

Start sleeves
L XXL
S M XL

12-row rep

Left edge st

10-stitch rep

Right edge st

| | Knit stitch on the right side/purl stitch on the wrong side

— Purl stitch on the right side/knit stitch on the wrong side

6.5 (6.5, 7, 7, 7.5)" / 16 (16, 17.5, 17.5, 19) cm

26 (26, 28, 28, 30) sts

6.25 (7.5, 8.5, 9.75, 10.75)" / 15.5 (19, 21, 24.5, 27) cm

25 (30, 34, 39, 43) sts

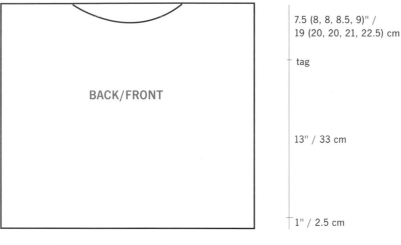

BACK/FRONT

7.5 (8, 8, 8.5, 9)" / 19 (20, 20, 21, 22.5) cm

tag

13" / 33 cm

1" / 2.5 cm

19 (21.5, 24, 26.5, 29)" / 47.5 (54, 60, 66.5, 72.5) cm

76 (86, 96, 106, 116) sts

Knit and purl stitches create a textured basketweave pattern.

Back

With the larger needle, cast on 76 (86, 96, 106, 116) stitches and work 7 rows of garter stitch. Continue in basket-weave pattern until the piece measures 14" (36 cm) from the cast-on edge. Place a stitch marker or yarn tag on each of the edge stitches to mark the beginning of the armhole. Work 7.5 (8, 8, 8.5, 9)" / 19 (20, 20, 22, 23) cm more in pattern. Either bind off or scrap off separately 25 (30, 34, 39, 43) stitches for each shoulder and 26 (26, 28, 28, 30) stitches for the center back neck.

Front

Work as for back to 6.75 (7.25, 7.25, 7.75, 8.25)" / 17 (18, 18, 20, 21) cm above armhole tags to begin shaping neckline. Work across 28 (33, 37, 42, 46) stitches, bind off the center 20 (20, 22, 22, 24) stitches and work to the end of the row. ★Working one side of the neckline, bind off at the neck edge 2 stitches once and 1 stitch once. Knit 1 more row and then bind off or scrap off the remaining 25 (30, 34, 39, 43) shoulder stitches.★★ Repeat from ★ to ★★ for the second shoulder.

Sleeves

Knit two sleeves alike, beginning the pattern for each size as shown on the stitch chart to ensure that the pattern is centered on the sleeve and keeping the first and last stitches as edge stitches. With the smaller needle, cast on 30 (32, 32, 34, 36) stitches and work 11 rows of garter stitch. Change to the larger needle and work 19" (48 cm) in pattern stitch, *at the same time* increasing 1 stitch at each end of every alternate row 0 (0, 0, 0, 2) times, every 4th row 20 (22, 22, 25, 24) times, and every 6th row 3 (2, 2, 0, 0) times. Work the increases as described on page 13.

When the sleeve measures 20.5" (52 cm) from the cast-on edge, bind off or scrap off 30 (32, 32, 34, 36) stitches at each end of the row, leaving 16 stitches at center for the shoulder strap. Continue working shoulder strap in pattern for 6.25 (7.5, 8.5, 9.75, 10.75)" / 16 (19, 22, 25, 27) cm, maintaining two plain knit stitches at each edge.

Finishing

Lightly block garment pieces from the wrong side. Join front and back shoulder seams to each shoulder strap. Sew sleeve and side seams, leaving 3" (8 cm) open for slits at the lower edge. With smaller (circular) needle and MC, pick up 26 (26, 28, 28, 30) stitches from the back neck, 16 stitches from first shoulder strap, 3 stitches along one side of front neckline, 20 (20, 22, 22, 24) stitches from the center front, 3 stitches from second side of front neckline, and 16 stitches from second shoulder strap. Work 7 rounds of garter stitch, working first round with purl stitches on right side. On the second round and every knit round, knit 2 stitches together at each of the seams (where shoulders and straps are joined). Bind off using the larger needle. Work in all yarn tails.

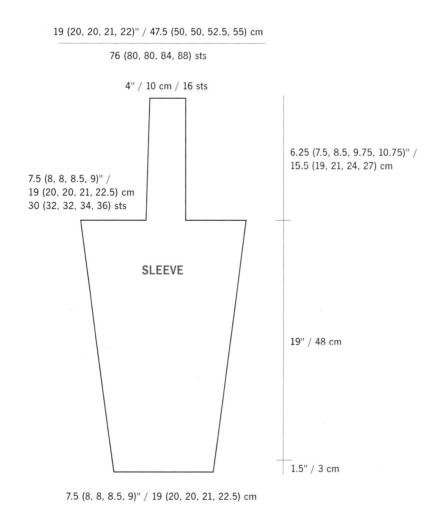

19 (20, 20, 21, 22)" / 47.5 (50, 50, 52.5, 55) cm

76 (80, 80, 84, 88) sts

4" / 10 cm / 16 sts

7.5 (8, 8, 8.5, 9)" /
19 (20, 20, 21, 22.5) cm
30 (32, 32, 34, 36) sts

6.25 (7.5, 8.5, 9.75, 10.75)" /
15.5 (19, 21, 24, 27) cm

SLEEVE

19" / 48 cm

1.5" / 3 cm

7.5 (8, 8, 8.5, 9)" / 19 (20, 20, 21, 22.5) cm

30 (32, 32, 34, 36) sts

purple sage

This garment's simple shaping—and the wide range of sizes offered here—make this sweater a perfect choice for everyone in the family.

Featured Design Variations

- Modified drop shoulder silhouette
- No neck shaping
- Boxy, oversized fit

Yarn: Adrienne Vitadini "Lucia" 53% wool, 47% cotton with 94 yards (86 meter) per 1.75 ounce (50 gram) ball, 12 (15, 17, 20, 23, 26) balls color #8412

Needles: Size US 7 (4.5 mm) straight or 29" (74 cm) circular needles and size 7 (4.5 mm) 16" (40 cm) for collar OR SIZE TO OBTAIN GAUGE

Notions: tape measure, tapestry needle

Gauge: 20 stitches and 32 rows = 4" (10 cm) in pattern stitch

Sizes: Women's XS (S, M, L, XL, XXL). Model is wearing size M.

Finished Measurements

Chest measurement: 35 (41, 44, 49.5, 52.5, 55)" / 89 (104, 112, 126, 133, 140) cm

Garment length: 22 (23, 25, 26, 28, 30)" / 56 (58, 64, 66, 71, 76) cm

Center back to cuff: 27.75 (29, 30, 31.25, 31.75, 32.75" / 70 (74, 76, 79, 81, 83) cm

Notes:

(1) All garment pieces are knitted with 2 knit stitches at each edge. All increasing/decreasing is done inside of these two stitches. (2) The main pattern is an extension of the rib, with garter stitch between the tucks and purls. (3) Wash and dry the swatch before measuring to allow for shrinkage and wash the finished garment. (4) Make sure you bind off the neckline and sleeve strap stitches so that they support the weight of the sweater, or, with an open collar and live stitches, the neckline might stretch out of shape.

Stitch Chart

Knit stitch on the right side/purl stitch on the wrong side

Purl stitch on the right side/knit stitch on the wrong side

Tuck stitch: Knit the stitch in row 1 (and all odd rows). Row 2 (and all even rows), insert the right needle into the stitch one row below, as if to purl.

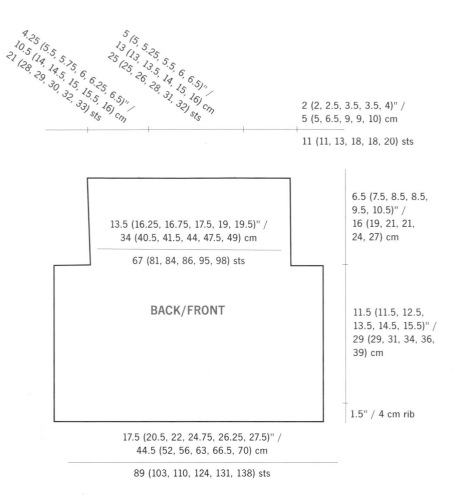

4.25 (5.5, 5.75, 6, 6.25, 6.5)" /
10.5 (14, 14.5, 15, 15.5, 16) cm /
21 (28, 29, 30, 32, 33) sts

5 (5, 5.25, 5.5, 6, 6.5)" /
13 (13, 13.5, 14, 15, 16) cm
25 (25, 26, 28, 31, 32) sts

2 (2, 2.5, 3.5, 3.5, 4)" /
5 (5, 6.5, 9, 9, 10) cm

11 (11, 13, 18, 18, 20) sts

6.5 (7.5, 8.5, 8.5, 9.5, 10.5)" /
16 (19, 21, 21, 24, 27) cm

13.5 (16.25, 16.75, 17.5, 19, 19.5)" /
34 (40.5, 41.5, 44, 47.5, 49) cm

67 (81, 84, 86, 95, 98) sts

BACK/FRONT

11.5 (11.5, 12.5, 13.5, 14.5, 15.5)" /
29 (29, 31, 34, 36, 39) cm

1.5" / 4 cm rib

17.5 (20.5, 22, 24.75, 26.25, 27.5)" /
44.5 (52, 56, 63, 66.5, 70) cm

89 (103, 110, 124, 131, 138) sts

Back/Front

Knit two pieces alike. Cast on 89 (103, 110, 124, 131, 138) stitches and work rib for 1.5" (4 cm). Continue in pattern stitch until piece measures 13 (13, 14, 15, 16, 17)" / 33 (33, 36, 38, 41, 43) cm from the cast-on edge. At the beginning of the next two rows, bind off 11 (11, 13, 18, 18, 20) stitches. 67 (81, 84, 88, 95, 98) stitches remain. Work straight for 6.5 (7.5, 8.5, 8.5, 9.5, 10.5)" / 17 (19, 22, 22, 24, 27) cm and then separately scrap off/bind off 21 (28, 29, 30, 32, 33) stitches for each shoulder and bind off the center 25 (25, 26, 28, 31, 32) stitches for the neckline.

Sleeves

Knit two alike, beginning and ending with 2 knit stitches and then the rib/pattern between as shown on the stitch chart. Cast on 46 stitches and work 1.5" (4 cm) rib. Work in pattern for 17.5" (45 cm), *at the same time* increasing 1 stitch at each end of every 8th row 3 (0, 0, 0, 0, 0) times, every 6th row 19 (15, 5, 5, 0, 0) times, every 4th row 0 (12, 27, 27, 32, 27) times, and every alternate row 0 (0, 0, 0, 5, 15) times. 90 (100, 110, 110, 120, 130) stitches. Tag the edge stitches to mark the beginning of the armholes, then work straight for 2 (2, 2.5, 3.5, 3.5, 4)" / 5 (5, 6, 9, 9, 10) cm. At the beginning of the next 2 rows, bind off 33 (38, 43, 43, 48, 53) stitches. 24 stitches remain. Work 4.25 (5.5, 5.75, 6, 6.25, 6.5)" / 11 (14, 15, 15, 16, 17) cm straight, slipping the first stitch, knitting the last, and working all other stitches as established in pattern. Bind off all 24 stitches.

The tuck-rib collar rolls softly away from the neckline.

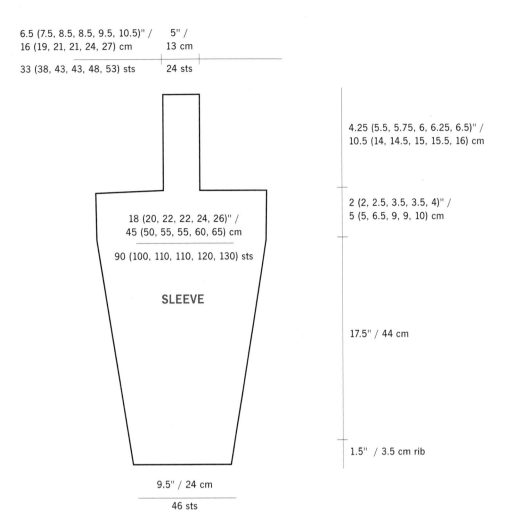

6.5 (7.5, 8.5, 8.5, 9.5, 10.5)" / 16 (19, 21, 21, 24, 27) cm

33 (38, 43, 43, 48, 53) sts

5" / 13 cm

24 sts

4.25 (5.5, 5.75, 6, 6.25, 6.5)" / 10.5 (14, 14.5, 15, 15.5, 16) cm

2 (2, 2.5, 3.5, 3.5, 4)" / 5 (5, 6.5, 9, 9, 10) cm

18 (20, 22, 22, 24, 26)" / 45 (50, 55, 55, 60, 65) cm

90 (100, 110, 110, 120, 130) sts

SLEEVE

17.5" / 44 cm

1.5" / 3.5 cm rib

9.5" / 24 cm

46 sts

Finishing

Block lightly. Join front shoulders to side edges of shoulder straps. Then join the side of the front armhole to the top of sleeve and the bound-off edge of the armhole to the side of sleeve, matching the armhole tag on the sleeve to the beginning of the garment armhole. Repeat for the back. Sew the sleeve and side seams.

For the neckband, with the smaller needle and the right side of the garment facing you, begin picking up stitches at center front. Pick up 13 stitches from the right front, 20 from the right shoulder strap, 23 (23, 26, 26, 29, 29) from the back neck, 20 from the left shoulder strap, and 13 from the left front. The collar will be worked back and forth over these stitches, not in the round.

Work the first row of the collar with the wrong side of the garment facing you, starting (k1, p1, k1) at the edge and then continuing (p2k1) and ending (p1k1) at the other edge. The second and all other right side rows are worked by knitting the knit stitches and tucking the purls. When collar measures 4" (10 cm), bind off loosely.

Work in all tails and wash the finished sweater.

back in the saddle again

The saddle drops to the back of this cardigan to create an unusual accent. Both the k6p2 rib and the k6p2 seeded rib are worked on the same size needle, so the sweater has nice straight lines.

Featured Design Variations

- Drop–shoulder silhouette
- Seeded rib patterning
- Back yoke detail

Yarn: Jamieson's Shetland Heather "Aran Knitting" 100% pure Shetland wool with 100 yards (92 meter) per 1.75 ounce (50 gram) ball, 10 (12, 14, 16, 18) balls "Gingersnap," #331

Needles: Size US 8 (5 mm) OR SIZE TO OBTAIN GAUGE

Notions: tape measure; tapestry needle; crochet hook, size F-H for finishing; 3 buttons: JHB #80331 (Dark Amber), 1.25" (3 cm)

Gauge: 17 stitches and 26 rows = 4" (10 cm) over seeded rib pattern

Sizes: Women's XS (S, M, L, XL). Model is wearing size M.

Finished Measurements

Chest measurement: 38 (42, 45, 49, 54)" / 97 (107, 116, 124, 135) cm

Garment length: 22.5 (24, 25.25, 26.5, 28)" / 57 (61, 64, 67, 71) cm

Center back to cuff: 28.5 (29.5, 30.25, 31.25, 32.25)" / 72 (75, 77, 79, 82) cm

Notes:

(1) Begin each garment piece as indicated on the chart for your size. (2) Work all increasing and decreasing 2 stitches from the edge, retaining 2 plain edge stitches. (3) The fronts are longer than the back to compensate for the saddle strap. The sleeves have a definite front/back armhole to accommodate this and must be knitted in reverse. It is a good idea to mark the back armhole stitches on each sleeve with a safety pin.

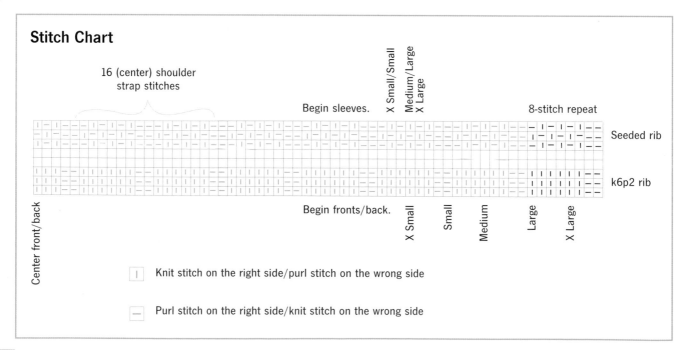

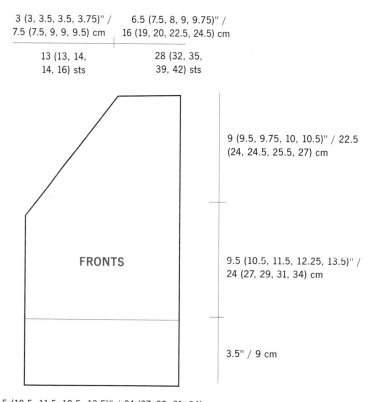

6 (6, 6.5, 6.5, 7.5)" / 15 (15, 16, 16, 19) cm

6.5 (7.5, 8, 9, 9.75)" / 16 (19, 20, 22.5, 24.5) cm

26 (26, 28, 28, 32) sts

28 (32, 35, 39, 42) sts

6 (6.5, 6.75, 7, 7.5)" / 15 (16, 16.5, 17.5, 19) cm

BACK

9.5 (10.5, 11.5, 12.5, 13.5)" / 24 (27, 29, 31, 34) cm

3.5" / 9 cm

19 (21, 22.5, 24.5, 27)" / 47.5 (52.5, 56.5, 61.5, 67.5) cm

82 (90, 98, 106, 116) sts

3 (3, 3.5, 3.5, 3.75)" / 7.5 (7.5, 9, 9, 9.5) cm

6.5 (7.5, 8, 9, 9.75)" / 16 (19, 20, 22.5, 24.5) cm

13 (13, 14, 14, 16) sts

28 (32, 35, 39, 42) sts

9 (9.5, 9.75, 10, 10.5)" / 22.5 (24, 24.5, 25.5, 27) cm

FRONTS

9.5 (10.5, 11.5, 12.25, 13.5)" / 24 (27, 29, 31, 34) cm

3.5" / 9 cm

9.5 (10.5, 11.5, 12.5, 13.5)" / 24 (27, 29, 31, 34) cm

41 (45, 49, 53, 58) sts

Back

Cast on 82 (90, 98, 106, 116) stitches and, beginning as indicated on the chart, work k6p2 rib for 3.5" (9 cm). Continue with k6p2 seeded rib pattern until piece measures 19 (20.5, 21.75, 23, 24.5)" / 48 (52, 55, 58, 62) cm from the cast-on edge, *at the same time* tagging the beginning of the armhole when the piece measures 13 (14, 15, 16, 17)" / 33 (36, 38, 41, 43) cm from the cast-on edge. Loosely scrap off/bind off all 82 (90, 98, 106, 116) stitches.

Fronts

Make two with reversed shaping. Cast on 41 (45, 49, 53, 58) stitches and work k6p2 rib as for back until the piece measures 13 (14, 15, 16, 17)" / 33 (36, 38, 41, 43) cm from the cast-on edge. Tag both edge stitches to mark the beginning of the armhole at one side and the beginning of the neck shaping at the other. The neck edge tags are used later when shaping the shawl collar.

At the front neck edge only, bind off 1 stitch at the beginning of the next row and every following 6th row 2 (4, 1, 3, 1) times, then every 4th row 10 (8, 12, 10, 14) times. When piece measures 22 (23.5, 24.75, 26, 27.5)" / 56 (60, 63, 66, 70) cm from the cast on edge, scrap off/bind off remaining 28 (32, 35, 39, 42) stitches.

Sleeves

Knit two with reverse shaping. Cast on 38 (38, 42, 42, 44) stitches and work 3.5" (9 cm) k6p2 rib. Continue in seeded rib pattern *at the same time* increasing 1 stitch at each end of every 6th row 5 (2, 4, 2, 0) times and every 4th row 17 (22, 19, 22, 25) times until the sleeve measures 19" (48 cm) from the cast-on edge. Loosely scrap off/bind off 25 (27, 28, 30, 33) stitches at the beginning of the next row. Work pattern across next 16 stitches and scrap off/bind off the remaining 41 (43, 44, 44, 45) stitches.

Work the shoulder strap for 9.5 (10.5, 11.25, 12.25, 13.25)" / 24 (27, 29, 31, 34) cm and then scrap off/slip to holder all 16 stitches.

Finishing

Lightly block all pieces. Join the top of both shoulder straps by grafting (page 23) or with another seaming method. Join the upper back to the back edge of the shoulder strap (the shorter depth armhole). Then sew the back armhole seams.

On the remaining edge of the shoulder strap, measure 6.5 (7.5, 8, 9, 9.75)" / 17 (19, 20, 23, 25) cm from each shoulder edge to mark the shoulders and neck. Join the front shoulder stitches to each end of the strap, then sew the front armhole seams.

Sew the sleeve and side seams of the garment. With the right side of the garment facing you, and beginning at the lower right front neckline edge, pick up 56 (60, 64, 68, 72) stitches along the right front edge up to the tag marking the beginning of the neckline. Pick up 42 stitches between the tag and the shoulder, 30 stitches across the back neck (double stitches as necessary), 42 along second side of neckline, and 56 (60, 64, 68, 72) along left front edge. Work k6p2 rib, *beginning with p2 (k4, p2, k4, p2)*. This should place k6 just before the neck shaping and just before the shoulder seam on both front edges. Work 4 rows of rib, making 3 evenly spaced 2-stitch buttonholes (pages 47 and 85) in the right front.

The shawl collar is shaped with short rows (page 17). Work row 5 from lower left edge to right neck tag. Wrap, turn, and work back to left neck tag. Wrap, turn, and work 8 stitches fewer each row 12 times until there are only 18 stitches working. Knit the next row all the way to the bottom of the right edge and the following row across all stitches, *taking care to knit the wraps with the stitches they encircle.* Work 4 more rows of rib. Loosely bind off.

Work in all yarn ends. Sew buttons to left front. Because Shetland looks its best once it has been washed, wash the finished sweater and lay it flat to dry.

The shoulder straps continue and meet at center back.

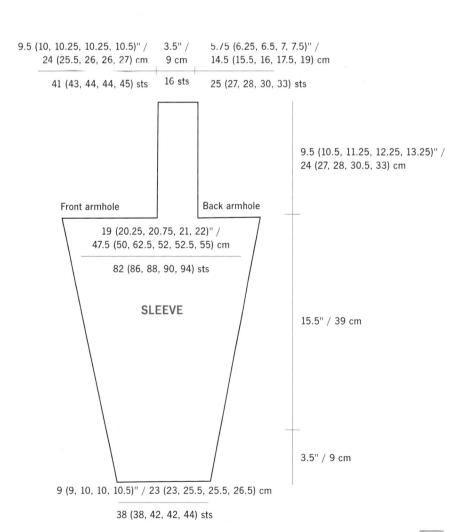

9.5 (10, 10.25, 10.25, 10.5)" / 24 (25.5, 26, 26, 27) cm   3.5" / 9 cm   5.75 (6.25, 6.5, 7, 7.5)" / 14.5 (15.5, 16, 17.5, 19) cm

41 (43, 44, 44, 45) sts   16 sts   25 (27, 28, 30, 33) sts

9.5 (10.5, 11.25, 12.25, 13.25)" / 24 (27, 28, 30.5, 33) cm

Front armhole   Back armhole

19 (20.25, 20.75, 21, 22)" / 47.5 (50, 62.5, 52, 52.5, 55) cm

82 (86, 88, 90, 94) sts

SLEEVE

15.5" / 39 cm

3.5" / 9 cm

9 (9, 10, 10, 10.5)" / 23 (23, 25.5, 25.5, 26.5) cm

38 (38, 42, 42, 44) sts

tumbleweeds

These vests are in two different styles, but both are worked in the same stitch pattern. One has a contemporary look. The other is more traditional, and could be worn by either a man or a woman.

Featured Design Variations

- Sleeveless silhouette
- Asymmetrical women's vest, with back color, integrally knitted button tabs, and no neck shaping
- False watch pocket in men's vest

Yarn: Schuler & Company "Schulana Tweed-Lux" 85% virgin wool, 10% silk, 5% cashmere with 110 yards (100 meter) per 1.75 ounce (50 gram) ball, 5 (7, 7, 8, 9) balls color #09 for women's vest OR 7 (8, 10, 10, 11) balls color #06 for men's vest

Needles: Size US 5 (3.75 mm) and US 7 (4.5 mm) straight or circular needles and US 5 (3.75 mm) 16" (41 cm) circular needle for armholes OR SIZE TO OBTAIN GAUGE

Notions: tape measure; tapestry needle; yarn markers; buttons: 3 JHB #90481 1.25" (3 cm) antique gold for women's vest OR 5 JHB #90296 0.75" (2 cm) nickel/gold for men's vest.

Gauge: 20 stitches and 24 rows = 4" (10 cm) over pattern stitch on larger needle

Sizes: Women's S (M, L, XL, XXL). Model is wearing size L.

Men's S (M, L, XL, XXL). Model is wearing size M.

Women's Finished Measurements

Chest measurement: 34.25 (40.75, 42.25, 47.25, 50.5)" / 87 (104, 107, 120, 128) cm

Garment length: 20.5 (21.25, 21.5, 22.5, 23.25)" / 52 (54, 55, 57, 59) cm

Men's Finished Measurements

Chest measurement: 38.25 (41.5, 46.75, 47.5, 50.5)" / 97 (105, 119, 121, 128) cm

Garment length: 24 (25, 25.5, 26, 26.5)" / 61 (64, 65, 66, 67) cm

Notes:

(1) Always slip the first and knit the last stitch in every row. (2) Work all decreases 1 stitch from the edge. (3) Scrapping off (see page 20) is suggested to facilitate finishing. The right front neck/collar edge will be picked up and finished with rib that turns cleanly to the outside, where a bound-off edge would show a ridge. The shoulder strap stitches will continue into the back collar. (4) The first row of the pattern is a right side row. (5) See stitch chart for placement of k2p2 rib and k4p4 rib relative to each other.

Stitch Chart

4-row repeat

4-stitch repeat

Edge stitch

Edge stitch

| | Knit stitch on the right side/ purl stitch on the wrong side |

| — | Purl stitch on the right side/knit stitch on the wrong side |

Twisted stitch: Knit 2nd stitch on left needle and then knit first stitch. Release both stitches from left needle.

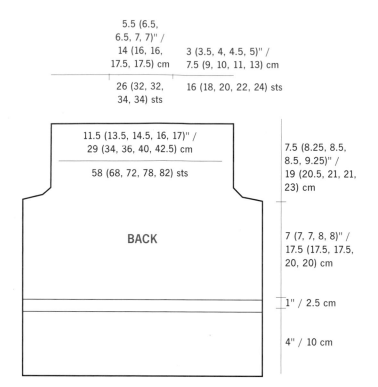

5.5 (6.5, 6.5, 7, 7)" / 14 (16, 16, 17.5, 17.5) cm

26 (32, 32, 34, 34) sts

3 (3.5, 4, 4.5, 5)" / 7.5 (9, 10, 11, 13) cm

16 (18, 20, 22, 24) sts

11.5 (13.5, 14.5, 16, 17)" / 29 (34, 36, 40, 42.5) cm

58 (68, 72, 78, 82) sts

7.5 (8.25, 8.5, 8.5, 9.25)" / 19 (20.5, 21, 21, 23) cm

BACK

7 (7, 7, 8, 8)" / 17.5 (17.5, 17.5, 20, 20) cm

1" / 2.5 cm

4" / 10 cm

16.75 (20, 21.5, 23.25, 25)" / 41.5 (50, 54, 58, 62.5) cm

84 (100, 108, 116, 124) sts

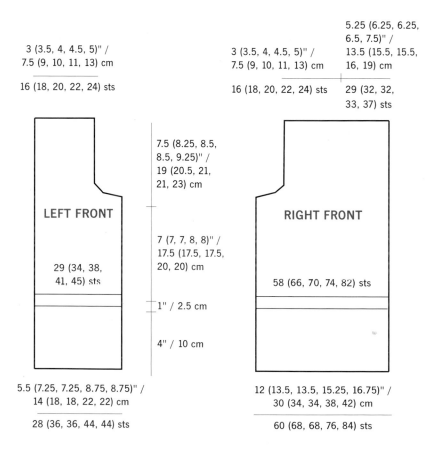

3 (3.5, 4, 4.5, 5)" / 7.5 (9, 10, 11, 13) cm

16 (18, 20, 22, 24) sts

3 (3.5, 4, 4.5, 5)" / 7.5 (9, 10, 11, 13) cm

16 (18, 20, 22, 24) sts

5.25 (6.25, 6.25, 6.5, 7.5)" / 13.5 (15.5, 15.5, 16, 19) cm

29 (32, 32, 33, 37) sts

7.5 (8.25, 8.5, 8.5, 9.25)" / 19 (20.5, 21, 21, 23) cm

LEFT FRONT

29 (34, 38, 41, 45) sts

7 (7, 7, 8, 8)" / 17.5 (17.5, 17.5, 20, 20) cm

1" / 2.5 cm

4" / 10 cm

RIGHT FRONT

58 (66, 70, 74, 82) sts

5.5 (7.25, 7.25, 8.75, 8.75)" / 14 (18, 18, 22, 22) cm

28 (36, 36, 44, 44) sts

12 (13.5, 13.5, 15.25, 16.75)" / 30 (34, 34, 38, 42) cm

60 (68, 68, 76, 84) sts

Women's Vest

Back

With the smaller needle, cast on 84 (100, 108, 116, 124) stitches and work k4p4 rib for 4" (10 cm). Then work k2p2 rib for 1" (2.5 cm). Change to larger needle and work pattern stitch until piece measures 12 (12, 12, 13, 13)" / 30 (30, 30, 33, 33) cm from cast-on edge.

Shape armholes by binding off at the beginning of the row 5 (5, 6, 6, 7) stitches twice, and 3 (3, 4, 4, 4) stitches twice, and 2 stitches 2 (4, 6, 6, 6) times. Then bind off 1 stitch at each end of every other row 3 (4, 2, 3, 4) times. 58 (68, 72, 78, 82) stitches remain.

Work straight until armhole measures 7.5 (8.25, 8.5, 8.5, 9.25)" / 19 (21, 22, 22, 23) cm. Separately scrap off 16 (18, 20, 22, 24) stitches for each shoulder and 26 (32, 32, 34, 34) stitches for the back neck.

Right Front

Cast on 60 (68, 68, 76, 84) stitches and work ribs as for back, increasing 2 (0, 2, 0, 0) OR decreasing 2 (2, 0, 2, 2) stitches evenly across first row of k2p2 rib. 58 (66, 70, 74, 82) stitches.

Shape armhole at left edge same as for back and continue until front is same length as back. Scrap off 16 (18, 20, 22, 24) stitches for the shoulder and 29 (32, 32, 33, 37) stitches for the front neck/collar.

Left Front

Cast on 28 (36, 36, 44, 44) stitches and work as for other pieces, evenly increasing 0 (0, 0, 2, 2) OR decreasing 2 (2, 2, 0, 0) stitches across first row of k2p2 rib. Work armhole at right edge. Work remaining 16 (18, 20, 22, 24) stitches until left front is the same length as right front. Scrap off the shoulder stitches.

Shoulder Straps

Knit two alike. Cast on 12 stitches. Maintain 1 plain stitch on each edge and work k2p2 rib between them for 3 (3.5, 4, 4.5, 5)" / 7 (9, 10, 11, 13) cm and then scrap off.

Finishing

Block all pieces lightly. Sew edges of shoulder straps to back shoulders, positioning the cast-on edge of the strap at the armhole edge of the garment and taking care to ensure that the right side of the strap begins and ends with k2. Sew front shoulders to shoulder straps, keeping right front neck/collar stitches free. Sew side seams.

Armhole bands: With the 16" (40 cm) needle and beginning at the side seam, with the right side of the garment facing you, pick up 36 (40, 40, 40, 44) stitches from the front armhole edge, 10 stitches from the strap, and 38 (42, 42, 42, 46) stitches from the back armhole edge. Work 5 rounds of k2p2 rib, double-checking when you reach the shoulder strap that the strap stitches continue perfectly into the band. Bind off loosely.

Left front band and back collar: With the right side facing you and beginning at the right front shoulder edge, pick up 10 stitches from the shoulder strap (doubling the first stitch of the 12-stitch strap), 26 (32, 32, 34, 34) back neck stitches, 10 shoulder strap stitches, and 64 (68, 68, 72, 76) stitches from the left front edge. Work k2p2 rib for 6 rows, reducing the back neck stitches to 22 (26, 26, 30, 30) in the first row. At the beginning of the 7th row, bind off all 64 (68, 68, 72, 76) front edge stitches, then work to the end of the row. Work 0.5" (1.3 cm) farther with k2p2 rib and then

The right front folds down to create a self-collar.

	I	I	I	I				I	I	I	I
		I	I	I	I				I	I	I	I
			I	I	I	I				I	I	I	I
I	I				I	I		I	I				I	I
I	I				I	I		I	I				I	I
I	I				I	I		I	I				I	I

To ensure that the edges of the collar match, when merging from k2p2 rib into k4p4 rib for the back collar, the groups of k4 stitches should center over the p2 stitches when you begin with knit 3 (1, 1, 3, 3) and then continue alternating p4 and k4

The button tabs are extensions of the front band.

3.5" (9 cm) of k4p4 rib, beginning with k3 (1, 1, 3, 3) followed by p4k4.

Right front band: With the right side facing you, pick up 68 (72, 72, 76, 80) stitches along right front edge and work k2p2 rib for 5 rows. At the beginning of the 6th row, bind off 14 (14, 14, 16, 16) stitches.

Buttonhole tab: Knit 6 rows rib back and forth over the next 6 stitches. In the 7th row make an eyelet buttonhole, as described in the box below. Work 3 more rows and bind off these 6 stitches and break the yarn. (Re-attach the yarn at the base of the tab just knitted and bind off the next 8 (8, 8, 10, 10) front edge stitches, then work the buttonhole tab on the next 6 stitches twice.) Bind off the remaining 20 (24, 24, 22, 26) front edge stitches.

Pick up 2 stitches from the top edge of the right front band and all 29 (32, 32, 33, 37) right front neck/collar stitches (from scrap). Work 5 rows of k2p2 rib and bind off loosely.

Work in all tails. Sew buttons to left front.

One-Stitch Eyelet Buttonholes

One-stitch eyelet buttonholes are the simplest buttonholes of all. Just knit 2 stitches together, followed by a yarn over. Work the yarn over as a stitch in the next row and the buttonhole is complete.

For slightly bigger buttons, you can make a two-stitch eyelet buttonhole by knitting 2 stitches together, followed by 2 yarn overs. Then slip 1, knit 1, and pass the slipped stitch over. In the next row, work the first yarn over through the front loop and the second yarn over through the back.

Men's Vest

Back

With the smaller needle, cast on 94 (102, 114, 118, 122) stitches and work k2p2 rib for 2" (5 cm). Change to the larger needle and work pattern stitch until piece measures 15" (38 cm) from the cast-on edge.

Shape armholes by binding off at the beginning of the following rows 5 stitches twice, 4 stitches 0 (0, 2, 2, 2) times, 3 stitches twice, 2 stitches twice, and 1 stitch 2 (2, 4, 4, 6) times. 72 (80, 82, 86, 88) stitches remain. Work straight until armhole measures 7.5 (8.5, 9, 9.5, 10)" / 19 (22, 23, 24, 25) cm. Separately bind off/scrap off or place on holders. 23 (27, 27, 29, 30) stitches for each shoulder and bind off 26 (26, 28, 28, 28) for back neck.

Fronts

Knit two with reverse shaping for left and right fronts. With smaller needle, cast on 46 (50, 58, 58, 62) stitches and work as for back until front measures 12" (30 cm) from cast-on edge. Place a marker on the front edge to mark beginning of neckline. Working 2 stitches from the front edge, decrease 1 stitch every other row 0 (0, 2, 0, 0) times, every 4th row 12 (9, 13, 9, 15) times and every 6th row 0 (3, 0, 4, 0) times, *at the same time* shaping the armhole as for the back when the piece measures 13" (33 cm) from the cast-on edge. Continue shaping neckline at one edge and armhole at the other as needed, then work neckline alone and work piece straight until armhole measures 7.5 (8.5, 9, 9.5, 10)" / 19 (22, 23, 24, 25) cm. Bind off/scrap off remaining 23 (27, 27, 29, 30) shoulder stitches.

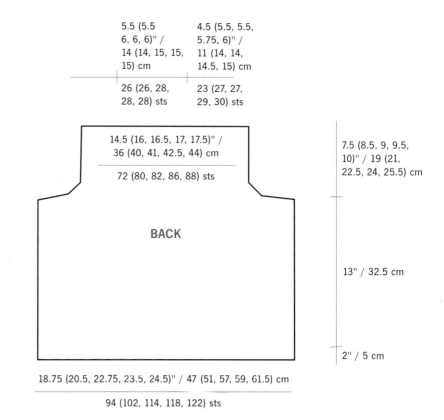

5.5 (5.5, 6, 6, 6)" / 14 (14, 15, 15, 15) cm

26 (26, 28, 28, 28) sts

4.5 (5.5, 5.5, 5.75, 6)" / 11 (14, 14, 14.5, 15) cm

23 (27, 27, 29, 30) sts

14.5 (16, 16.5, 17, 17.5)" / 36 (40, 41, 42.5, 44) cm

72 (80, 82, 86, 88) sts

7.5 (8.5, 9, 9.5, 10)" / 19 (21, 22.5, 24, 25.5) cm

BACK

13" / 32.5 cm

2" / 5 cm

18.75 (20.5, 22.75, 23.5, 24.5)" / 47 (51, 57, 59, 61.5) cm

94 (102, 114, 118, 122) sts

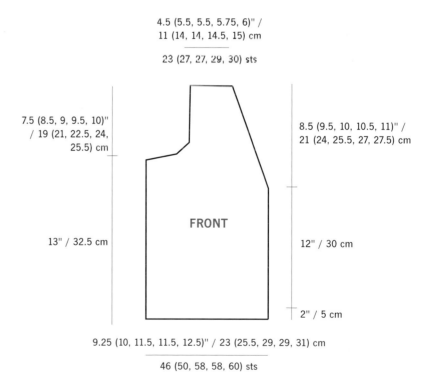

4.5 (5.5, 5.5, 5.75, 6)" / 11 (14, 14, 14.5, 15) cm

23 (27, 27, 29, 30) sts

7.5 (8.5, 9, 9.5, 10)" / 19 (21, 22.5, 24, 25.5) cm

8.5 (9.5, 10, 10.5, 11)" / 21 (24, 25.5, 27, 27.5) cm

FRONT

13" / 32.5 cm

12" / 30 cm

2" / 5 cm

9.25 (10, 11.5, 11.5, 12.5)" / 23 (25.5, 29, 29, 31) cm

46 (50, 58, 58, 60) sts

Shoulder Straps

With the smaller needle, cast on 20 stitches and work k2p2 rib, beginning and ending k3, for 4.5 (5.5, 5.5, 5.75, 6)" / 11 (14, 14, 15, 15) cm. Bind off/scrap off or place on holder.

Finishing

Lightly block all pieces. Sew back shoulders to edge of shoulder strap with cast-on edge of strap at armhole edge of garment and right side of strap, beginning k3. Sew front shoulder seams and side seams.

Armhole bands: With the smaller needle and the right side of the garment facing you, beginning at the side seam, pick up 80 (88, 96, 100, 100) stitches and work 8 rounds of k2p2 rib, then bind off loosely. When picking up stitches from the edge of the strap, do not pick up stitch for stitch; reduce the edge to 14 stitches or the strap will be too wide.

Neckband: With the smaller needle and the right side of the garment facing you, begin at the lower right edge. Pick up 66 stitches between lower edge and beginning of neckline, 34 (38, 42, 42, 46) stitches along right side of neckline, 20 stitches from (scrap) right shoulder strap, 18 stitches from back neck, 20 from left shoulder strap, 34 (38, 42, 42, 46) from left side of neckline, and 66 from left front edge. (If the center back neck stitches were held on a holder or scrap knitting, reduce to 18 stitches by knitting 2 stitches together every other stitch in the first row of the band.)

Work k2p2 rib for 3 rows. Row 4, make 2-stitch buttonholes (pages 47 and 85) in left front (for a man or right front for a woman). Place markers as follows: Each buttonhole will require 2 stitches, with the first one positioned 4 stitches from the lower edge and the remaining buttonholes 12 stitches apart. The top buttonhole should fall at the beginning of the neckline shaping. Work 4 more rows and then bind off.

False watch pocket: Cast on 20 stitches and work k2p2 rib for 1.5" (4 cm). Scrap off. Fold the scrap back and position the pocket on the left front. Hand-sew the main stitches to the garment and then remove the scrap yarn. Sew the sides of the pocket flap in place.

Work in all tails. Sew buttons opposite buttonholes.

One-Row Buttonholes

Buttonhole spacing is simple to work out if you remember that there are more spaces between, before, and after the buttons than there are buttons. So, if you plan to have three buttons, you need to plan for two equal spaces between the buttons and also two smaller spaces before the first and after the last button.

The first and last buttons on most cardigans are just a few stitches from the edge, and those spaces can often accommodate any extra rows left over from spacing the other buttons. On V-necklines, the top button is generally even with the beginning of the neck shaping. If you can knit the button band before you knit the buttonhole band, you can easily count out the rows or ribs and place safety pins where you think the buttons should go. For a band that is worked around the entire neckline, you have to count the ribs and spacing on the first few rows of the band that are knitted.

Remember that in addition to the spaces between them, each buttonhole will require 2 to 3 stitches for the buttonhole itself. Always work up a sample so you know exactly how many stitches you'll need to use to create a buttonhole that will be large enough for your button to pass through and snug enough to hold it there.

To knit a one-row buttonhole:

1. Knit to the beginning of the buttonhole and then bring the yarn to the front to slip the first stitch as if to purl, then put the yarn in back (slip 1, pass the first stitch over the second) two or three times, depending on the size of your button. Return the last stitch from the right needle to the left. Do not turn the work.

2. With the yarn in back, use the cable cast-on method to cast on one more stitch than you bound off in step 1. Turn the work.

3. With the yarn in back, slip the first stitch from the left needle to the right needle and then pass the last cast-on stitch over it. Continue working to the end of the row.

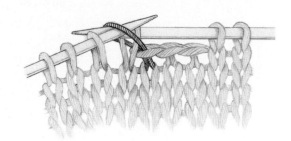

1

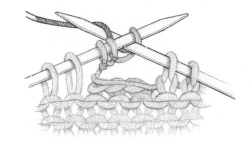

2

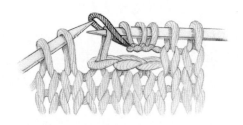

3

Knitting by Machine

All the sweaters in this book can be knitted by machine, either just as they are in the hand-knit instructions or with modifications. The machine-knitting instructions for twelve garments could be another, entire book, so I am providing just the most essential guidelines and am assuming you are familiar with your own knitting machine and have some experience using it. You may have other methods that you like to use, so don't feel that you have to do things exactly as I am suggesting.

Depending on your machine's gauge, you might have to use a different yarn than the one listed for the hand-knit pattern. Substituting yarns will require recharting unless you are using some kind of charting attachment. Not every sweater can be knitted on every machine—and not every sweater can be machine knitted exactly like the hand-knit version.

Although your machine may be the correct gauge for the yarn specified for a particular pattern, be aware that your bed may not have enough needles for some of the largest sizes. Generally, standard-gauge machines have 200 needles, mid-gauge have 150, and chunky/bulky machines 110, with minor variations from one brand to another. Each of these machines handles a very specific range of yarns. Chunky machines are slightly more able than the earlier bulky models to handle the heaviest yarns. Split Rails (page 38), Desert Dreams (page 44), and Square Dance (page 66) will require a ribber.

The hand-knit stitch counts are the same for machine knitting, but all inches must be converted to row counts. Knit a couple of gauge swatches to get as close as you can to the row gauge of the pattern. If you can't match the gauge, you will need to rechart. I can almost always match hand-knit gauges if I am persistent. Try the clicks between full-stitch sizes and adjust the tension mast. Of course, if you have a charting attachment, you just need to draw the schematic onto a sheet of scaled paper and use the stitch ruler that matches your gauge. You may also be able to rework the pattern with a computer charting program.

Work all increases and decreases one stitch from the edge to facilitate seaming and finishing. I usually prefer full-fashioned shaping, and it's up to you whether to use a 2-prong or 3-prong tool.

Please consult your knitting machine manual for operating directions specific to your machine. Many of the sweaters in this book will rely on hand manipulations, rather than automatic patterning, and my first book, *Hand-Manipulated Stitches for Machine Knitters* (Taunton Press,

1990), is full of ideas and information. (The book is currently out of print, but you can probably locate a copy through your local library or online booksellers.)

You will knit the back, front(s), and sleeves according to the specific directions for each pattern. I prefer scrapping off to binding off whenever possible. If you knit neckbands on the machine, do not join the last shoulder seam until the band is done. Most bands can be latched up, knitted with a ribber/double bed, or worked by hand.

A slick way to join the saddle straps to the front/back shoulder stitches is to rehang the side edge of a shoulder strap on the machine with the right side facing you. Bring the needles all the way forward and push the fabric back against the bed. With the wrong side facing you, hang the live front/back shoulder stitches into the hooks of the same needles. Close the latches and slowly push the needles back into working position so that the stitches are pulled through the edge of the fabric. Then bind off.

Machine Recommendations:

M = mid-gauge
B = bulky
C = chunky
S = standard
EONS = every other needle standard gauge

Note: Although many yarns will knit on every other needle of a standard-gauge machine, you will only have 100 needles to work with.

Pinto
Page 28
Machine: M, B, C, EONS
Patterning: Stockinette. Bands can be latched, worked on a ribber/double bed, or knitted by hand.

Rope Tricks
Page 32
Machine: M, B, C
Patterning: Lots and lots of cables to cross manually. If worked single-bed, you will also need to reform all the stitches between them. This is not an impossible sweater to knit by machine, but it will require patience and skill. Make sure the stitches are well weighted so the cables cross more easily.

Split Rails
Page 38
Machine: M, S with ribber
Patterning: Fisherman Rib (also called English Rib) is a snap to knit by machine, but you must have a ribber. Every ribber/double bed manual I have ever seen has directions for this stitch.

Desert Dreams
Page 44
Machine: M, B, C with ribber
Patterning: Even with a ribber, you will not be able to exactly duplicate this stitch because of the columns of seed stitch (stitches that alternately knit or purl) between the columns of knit and purl stitches. You could, however, produce a pretty good imitation using tuck stitches instead of seed stitches. The tuck stitches can be automatically formed or hand-pulled. Without a ribber, every 4th stitch will periodically need to be reformed.

OK Kids
Page 48

Machine: M, B, C

Patterning: The cables will need to be turned by hand and the purl stitches between them latched up unless you choose to knit this with a double bed/ribber.

Blue Bonnets
Page 54

Machine: M, B, C

Patterning: Twisted stitches are most easily done on a machine as follows: Remove a pair of stitches on a 2-prong transfer tool. Rotate the tool 180 degrees to the right and slip another 2-prong tool into the same stitches from the opposite direction. Remove the first tool and then replace the stitches on the needles. You can also use a pair of single-prong transfer tools and treat the stitches as 1x1 cables—but there are a lot of stitches, so this method would be much slower. The tuck stitches can be worked with automatic-punchcard or electronic patterning or by placing needles into holding position.

Rodeo
Page 58

Machine: M, B, C

Patterning: The color work will be simple to do on any machine, with or without automatic patterning. You will, however, need to use a garter bar to turn the work over every 4 rows unless you substitute another stitch for this row—I suggest tuck stitch.

Prairie
Page 62

Machine: M, B, C

Patterning: The children's version of this sweater is the only one in the book that was actually knitted by machine. I used a single bed Studio SK860, which is a 6.5 mm, mid-gauge machine. I knitted all the bands by hand and then hung them on the machine to continue knitting the garment pieces. The front and back were fast and simple to do—just plain stockinette. The sleeves required latching up the stitches on either side of the twisted stitches every 8 to 10 rows. Twisted stitches are simple to do on the machine. (See notes for Blue Bonnets on facing page.)

Square Dance
Page 66
Machine: M, B, C with ribber
Patterning: Basket weave requires you to continually transfer groups of stitches back and forth between the ribber (front) and the main (back) bed. You can do this manually, stitch by stitch, or locate some MT transfer tools that will transfer groups of 12 or more stitches at a time. Your machine may also have a ribber transfer carriage.

Purple Sage
Page 70
Machine: M, B, C
Patterning: The tuck stitch in this garment is not a problem for the knitting machine, but the garter stitch is. You need to substitute another pattern for the one in the hand-knit version—perhaps an automatic slipstitch pattern, combined with some hand-manipulated tuck stitches. If you have a standard-gauge machine with a garter carriage, you could knit this sweater exactly as shown, but with a lighter weight yarn.

Back in the Saddle Again
Page 74
Machine: M, B, C
Patterning: You'll need to substitute another texture stitch for the seed stitch unless you have a standard-gauge machine with garter carriage. In that case, you'll have to work with a much lighter weight yarn than in the hand-knit version.

Tumbleweeds
Page 78
Machine: M, B, C
Patterning: These vests require a lot of twisted stitches! It would probably not be practical to try reforming the stitches between them, so I would suggest a tuck-stitch pattern instead. Even if you do not have automatic-punchcard or electronic patterning, hand-pulling the tuck stitch is still faster than making an all-over twisted stitch fabric.

Glossary of Basic Techniques

Here are some of the basic techniques you'll need when working through the patterns in this book. I have also included some recommendations as to which techniques work best for particular sweaters. New knitters may find this glossary especially helpful. If you are a more experienced knitter, refer to it as needed.

Casting On and Binding Off

Most knitters have their favorite cast-on and bind-off methods. Unless your pattern specifies a particular method—to accommodate a specific yarn, technique, or finishing method—you can usually choose whichever you prefer. Here are some of the standards:

The simple looped cast-on is fast and easy, but often not suitable for visible edges. It tends to be somewhat slack and lacks elasticity, but it works just fine for swatching or when casting on stitches for buttonholes.

Simply wrap your finger with loops that resemble the lowercase letter "e" and then slip each loop onto the needle.

The long-tail cast-on is quick and produces a nice, firm edge. Be careful not to tighten each stitch too much. If you do, the first row will be difficult to knit and the edge may be too firm or draw in

the knitting. The long-tail cast-on is a good, all-purpose cast-on, although it's not a practical way to add body stitches.

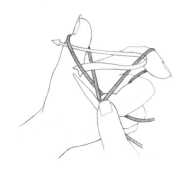

After each stitch is formed, you will have to reposition the "heart" on your left hand to make the next stitch. The process becomes faster and more automatic with each stitch.

To make a long-tail cast-on, pull out twice as much length as you think you'll need and make a slip knot around the needle. Now hold both the long tail and the continuous yarn in the palm of your left hand. (I usually pinch the two yarns with my little finger and my ring finger to create some tension.) Insert your thumb and index finger between the two yarns and move them away from each other so that the strands form a heart shape. *Scoop the tip of the needle under the left strand of the left side of the heart (from left to right) and then

over the left strand of the right side of the heart, pulling it through from right to left. Snug the stitch on the needle ★★ and repeat ★ to ★★.

The cable cast-on is another good, all-purpose cast-on. It works well for making one-row buttonholes or adding multiple stitches to a piece in progress. To keep the stitches from tightening too much, I insert my right needle into the space for the next stitch before tightening the previous one.

Make a slipknot on the left needle and knit it as a stitch, then place this new stitch on the left needle. ★Insert the right needle in the space behind the first stitch on the left needle and knit it as a stitch. Instead of dropping the stitch from the left needle or moving stitches to the right needle, the new loop is slipped onto the left needle.★★ Repeat from ★ to ★★ until enough stitches have been cast on.

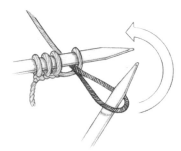

When slipping the new stitches onto the needle, be consistent in how you do or don't twist them so that the edge is uniform.

The most basic bind-off is all you'll need for the patterns in this book. Slip the first stitch, knit the next stitch, and then pass the slipped stitch over the knit stitch. Continue knitting one more stitch and passing the previous stitch over it until there is one stitch left or until you have bound off enough stitches and want to continue knitting on the remaining stitches. When binding off all the stitches, simply cut the yarn and pull it through the last stitch.

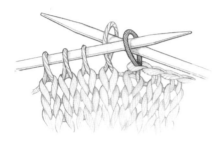

The key to this bind-off is to knit the stitches looser than usual, making sure they do not tighten as you pass over each slipped stitch.

The three-needle bind-off is used to join two sets of live stitches in a seam. The effect is much less bulky than it would be if you bound off both sets of stitches and then seamed them. Each set of stitches remains on a needle. (I will sometimes work this bind-off on stitches that I have scrapped off, first feeding them back onto needles.)

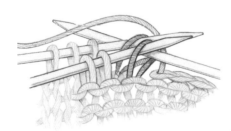

If you find it difficult to draw the yarn through two sets of stitches, try substituting a crochet hook for the third needle.

Hold the two needles in your left hand, with the right sides of the fabric together, and work a basic bind-off with a third needle. The only difference between the three-needle bind-off and the basic bind-off is that you insert the right needle through *two stitches* each time, one on each of the two left needles.

I-Cords

I-cords are versatile tubes that can be knitted on as few as 2 stitches, but usually on 3 or 4. They represent circular knitting at its smallest! I-cords make good ties, belts, and trimmings of all kinds. They can also be used as a bind-off method (see Rope Tricks, page 37). Two-stitch I-cords look square, 3- to 5-stitch cords look like round shoelaces, and wider cords start to flatten.

You work I-cords on two, short, double-pointed needles. Cast on 3 stitches and knit 1 row. Do not turn the work over. *Slide the knitting back to the beginning of the row, letting the yarn float across the back of the stitches, and knit 1 row. Do not turn.** Repeat from * to ** for the desired length. When you give the finished tube a good tug, the stitches realign themselves and absorb the little gaps that form when you carry the yarn across the back of the stitches to begin each row.

Increasing and Decreasing

There are many ways to increase and decrease. If you have methods that you prefer, please use them. When practical, I like to pair my increases and decreases so that they slant in the opposite directions at each edge of a sleeve or neckline. To maintain an even edge, remember to work increases and decreases at least one stitch from the edge of the fabric.

The following methods are for increasing or decreasing knit stitches on the right side of the fabric, but you can also work them on the purl side—simply substitute the word "purl" for "knit" in the directions.

Paired Increases

Left-slanting increase: Knit 1 stitch, then insert the left needle into the left loop of the stitch two rows below the stitch just knitted. Knit this loop as a stitch (or lift the loop onto the needle and then knit it). This increase will slant to the left.

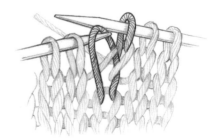

You may find it easier to knit the loop two rows below by lifting it onto the left needle first.

Right-slanting increase: Insert the right needle into the right loop of the stitch one row below the next stitch on the left needle, then knit this loop (or lift the loop onto the needle and then knit it) and the original stitch above it. This increase slants towards the right.

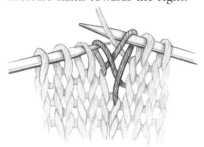

The loop one row below is knitted before the stitch above it.

Paired Decreases

The SKP decrease slants towards the left. Slip 1 stitch, knit 1 stitch, then pass the slipped stitch over the knit stitch.

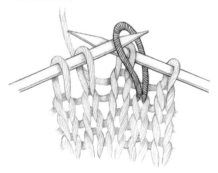

The slipped stitch should be slipped as if to knit.

The K2tog decrease slants towards the right. Insert the right needle into 2 stitches on the left needle and knit the 2 stitches together.

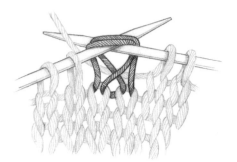

On the purl side of the fabric, this decrease is worked as purl 2 together.

Tuck Stitches

Tuck stitches are worked on either the knit side or the purl side of a fabric. To make them, insert the right needle into the stitch one row below on the left needle. The right needle can be inserted to knit or to purl, regardless of which side of the fabric faces you. Drop the stitch from the left needle, and a new stitch is formed in the lower stitch with the upper stitch sort of draped—or tucked—around it. The effect is different on each side of the knit fabric. This stitch forms the basis for Fisherman's Rib (Split Rails, page 38) and can provide interesting texture with other stitches, too (Blue Bonnets, page 54).

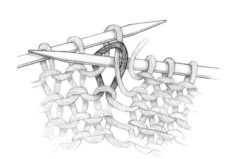

Tucking as if to purl

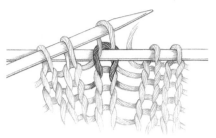

Tucking as if to knit

Twisted Stitches

Twisted stitches are first cousins to baby, 1×1 cables, and they are worked without a cable needle. Insert the right needle through the second stitch on the left needle as if to knit and in front of the first stitch. Knit the second stitch and then the first. When you release both stitches from the left needle, they will be crossed. There's a variation of this twisted stitch described in the instructions for Blue Bonnets on page 57.

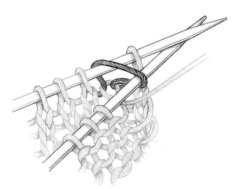

When working a twisted stitch, the second stitch on the left needle is knitted first and is not released from the needle until the first stitch has been knitted. The result is a 1x1 cable, knitted without a cable needle.

Sources of Supply

Berroco Inc.
14 Elmdale Road
Box 367
Uxbridge, MA 01569 USA
phone: (508) 278-2527
email: info@berroco.com
www.berroco.com

Cascade Yarns
www.cascadeyarns.com

Classic Elite Yarns Inc.
122 Western Avenue
Lowell, MA 01851 USA
phone: (978) 453-2837
www.classiceliteyarns.com

Golden Hands Industries
phone: (800) 998-1392
*Sure Block (36" × 54" gridded
blocking cloths)*

JCA Crafts Inc.
35 Scales Lane
Townsend, MA 01469-1094 USA
phone: (978) 597-8794
www.jcacrafts.com
Adrienne Vittadini yarns

JHB International Inc.
1955 South Quince Street
Denver, CO 80231 USA
phone: (303) 751-8100
(800) 525-9007
email: sales@buttons.com
www.buttons.com
*JHB buttons are available at most
retail stores.*

Knitting Fever Inc.
PO Box 336
Amityville, NY 11701 USA
phone: (516) 546-3600 /
(800) 645-3457
email:
knittingfever@knittingfever.com
www.knittingfever.com
Debbie Bliss yarns

Schuler & Company
(US Distribution)
Skacel Collection Inc.
PO Box 88110
Seattle, WA 98138 USA
phone: (425) 291-9600
(800) 255-1278
email: info@skacelknitting.com
www.skacelknitting.com

(European distribution)
Fachstrasse 21
Postfach
CH-8942 Oberrieden/ZH
SWITZERLAND
phone: +41 (0) 44723 15 00
email: info@lana.ch

www.schulana.ch
Addi Turbo Cro-Needle

Simply Shetland
10 Domingo Road
Santa Fe, NM 87508 USA
www.simplyshetland.net
Jamieson's yarns

Tahki/Stacy Charles Inc.
70-30 80th Street, Building 36
Ridgewood, NY 11385 USA
phone: (800) 338-YARN /
(800) 338-9276
email: info@tahkistacycharles.com
www.tahkistacycharles.com

Westminster Fibers Inc.
4 Townsend Avenue, Unit 8
Nashua, NH 03060 USA
phone: (603) 886-5041 / (800)
445-9276
email: linda.pratt@westminster-
fibers.com
www.westminsterfibers.com
Nashua Handknits and Rowan yarns

Woolstock Yarn Shop
(Blocking wires)
4876 Butler Road
Glyndon, MD 21071
phone: (410) 517-1020 /
(800) 242-5648
www.woolstock.com

Meet the Knitters

I'm fortunate to have some wonderful friends—and doubly lucky that so many of them are great knitters! I designed all the sweaters in this book, but I did not knit all of them. I hand-knit the boys' version of OK Kids (page 48) and the women's version of Tumbleweeds (page 78) and machine-knit the girls' version of Prairie (page 62). The other sweaters were hand-knitted by friends who are scattered all around the country. Knitters are usually the unsung heroes of most magazines and books, so I'd like to introduce you to my cadre of hand-knitting experts!

Laurencia Ciprus
Essex, Connecticut

I met Laurencia while I was working as the education director for a handcraft center in Guilford, Connecticut. She was one of the loyal volunteers who made the place tick! Coincidentally, her mother, who I knew only as "Sweater Rescue," was the woman who did all the knitting repair work for the yarn shop I ran with my sister-in-law for several years. Laurencia is a fast knitter, and she made three sweaters for this book: Blue Bonnets (page 54), Square Dance (page 66), and Purple Sage (page 70).

Jeanne Drury
Hamden, Connecticut

Jeanne was a customer at my yarn shop, Have You Any Wool?, and eventually she started teaching classes for us. She loves color work and cables and has the patience of a knitting saint, which is why she is such an excellent teacher—and one of the best knitters I know. An architect by day, Jeanne has a keen understanding of details and did a beautiful job knitting Rope Tricks (page 32).

Carol Marcarelli
North Haven, Connecticut

Carol is my sister-in-law and dear friend and also my former partner in our yarn shop, Have You Any Wool? She knits constantly, and I purposely sized OK Kids (page 48) to fit one of her granddaughters. Carol is an experienced knitter and an excellent teacher. She even taught her husband how to knit one winter when we were snowed in week after week!

Lynne McClune
East Sound, Washington

Lynne was a knitting educator when I worked for Studio by White Knitting Machines. She was one of the few machine knitters I knew who also knit by hand—and made it look just as fast and easy. When Lynne left Studio, she took on the job of coordinating the huge *Stitches* shows for *Knitters* magazine for several years. Lynne knitted the woman's version of Prairie (page 62) and Desert Dreams (page 44).

Brenda O'Brien
Wallingford, Connecticut

Brenda was one of my customers at the yarn shop and later an employee. A fast and excellent hand-knitter, she took to the machines immediately, which made her a great asset to the store. She's also one of the most positive people I know. Despite having several challenges in her life right now, she still had the time and energy to knit Pinto (page 28). Thanks, Brenda!

Kate Perri
White Plains, New York

Kate "picked me up" in the grocery store about 30 years ago. I was carrying a hand-woven shoulder bag that gave me away as a "fiber person." She spotted it right away. The next day, she came to visit my weaving studio and we've been friends ever since. Kate is also a quilter and sewer, and she knitted the man's version of Tumbleweeds (page 78) while she was working on her first book, *Easy Singer Style: Pattern-Free Fashions & Accessories* (Creative Publishing international, 2007).

Lisa Wolkow
Madison, Connecticut

Meeting Lisa was one of the best things about working at the Guilford Art Center. I always feel good when I'm with her. She is a brilliant ceramic artist and also one of the fastest, most even hand-knitters I have ever met. Lisa used to knit sample sweaters for some big-name fashion designers, so I was honored she agreed to knit Rodeo (page 58).

Gini Woodward
Bonners Ferry, Idaho

Gini is a well-known machine knitter and teacher. We became friends during my Studio by White days, and despite the fact that there is a whole country between us, we have remained close, constant friends. If we lived any closer, the energy we generate together would exhaust us! Both a hand-knitter and machine-knitter, Gini understands knits the same way that I do. I can always rely on her for good advice and feedback. She knitted Back in the Saddle Again (page 74) and Split Rails (page 38).

About the Author

Designer Susan Guagliumi has created original hand-knit and machine-knit garments and has written articles for *Vogue Knitting, Knitters, Family Circle Easy Knitting,* and other magazines. She is also the author of *Hand-Manipulated Stitches for Machine Knitters* (Taunton Press, 1990) and *Twelve Sweaters One Way: Knitting Cuff to Cuff* (Creative Publishing international, 2006). She wrote and hosted a series of instructional videos for Studio by White Knitting Machines. Susan lives in Northford, Connecticut, with her artist husband, Arthur.

Credits

Beautiful yarns make it easy to be inspired to design and knit beautiful garments! My sincere thanks to Berroco Inc.; Cascade Yarns; Classic Elite Yarns Inc.; JCA/Vittadini; KFI; Simply Shetland; Skacel Yarns; Tahki/Stacy Charles Inc.; and Westminster Fibers—and to JHB International Inc. for providing the final touches.

Special thanks to Margery Winter, Norah Gaughan, Andra Asars, Nancy Thomas, Jim Baldini, and Linda Pratt, who have been supportive in so many ways through the years.